# Happy Mealtimes

## for Kids

# About the author

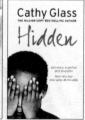

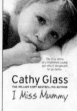

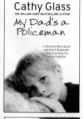

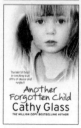

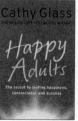
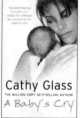

Bestselling author Cathy Glass, who writes under
a pseudonym, has been a foster carer for more
than twenty-five years. She has three children.
To find out more about Cathy and her story,
visit www.cathyglass.co.uk

# Cathy Glass

# Happy Mealtimes

## for Kids

### A Guide to Healthy Eating with Simple Recipes that Children Love

# HARPER

An imprint of HarperCollins*Publishers*
77–85 Fulham Palace Road,
Hammersmith, London W6 8JB

www.harpercollins.co.uk

First published by HarperCollins*Publishers* 2012

10 9 8 7 6 5 4 3 2 1

A catalogue record of this book is
available from the British Library

PB ISBN 978-0-00-749748-5
EB ISBN 978-0-00-749749-2

Printed and bound in Great Britain by
Clays Ltd, St Ives plc

**MIX**
Paper from
responsible sources
**FSC** **FSC™ C007454**
www.fsc.org

This book features recipe ideas which may not be suitable for everyone. This book
is not tailored to individual requirements, needs, sensitivities or allergies and is
solely for general information purposes. Nothing contained in this book should be
taken as professional advice and it should not be used as a substitute for any
meal plan, advice or treatment prescribed by your doctor. The author and
publisher do not accept any responsibility for adverse effects that may occur as a
result of the use of the suggestions or information herein. If you feel that you are
experiencing any adverse effects, sensitivities or allergies after trying any new
foods or meal regime you should seek professional medical advice.

# Contents

# Introduction: Why happy mealtimes?

I am a foster carer, and as well as bringing up three children of my own, I have looked after other people's children for over twenty-five years. Some of those children stayed with me for a few days, while others stayed for years. The reasons why children come into care vary – from a single parent having to go into hospital for a night, to a child being badly neglected and abused. While some of the children I've fostered had received adequate diets at home, the vast majority – over 95 per cent – had not, resulting in the children being under- or overweight, short in stature, with dull skin and hair, lacking energy, and often having difficulties in concentrating and therefore being behind with their learning.

One of the first changes I have to make when a child comes to live with me is to their diet, and they are often resistant to change. When the children have been used to snacking on whatever was to hand – usually crisps and biscuits – not only do I have to wean them on to 'proper' food but also I have to introduce them to mealtimes rather than having snacks in front of the television. Highly processed food – usually the only food they have known – is often visually attractive and easy to eat (requiring hardly any chewing), but it has few nutrients and addictive amounts of salt and sugar. I have to win the children over to a healthier way of eating as well as providing meals that the whole family enjoys, and like most busy parents I don't have much time. I have therefore become adept at producing simple nutritious meals that are easy to make and which kids of all ages will love. In this book I share my recipes, together with some important food facts. I hope you find it useful. *Bon appétit*.

# CHAPTER ONE

# What is a bad diet for kids?

No food is actually 'bad' for a child, unless it is poisonous or the child is allergic to it, or is on a restrictive diet, but some foods become 'bad' because of the quantity in which they are eaten. A poor diet is usually high in sugar and fat, low in protein, and lacking in vitamins and minerals. So, for example, a packet of crisps in a lunch box alongside a sandwich containing protein (such as meat, fish or eggs) and a piece of fruit is fine, but four packets of crisps a day are not, especially when they replace a meal. Likewise a piece of chocolate or a cup cake in addition to a main meal is acceptable, but chocolate and cake regularly eaten in large quantities are not. Crisps, chocolate and most heavily processed snack foods are high in calories, salt, sugar and fat, and low in nutrients, so must be eaten in moderation.

You may find it incredible that a child could ever be given chocolate or crisps instead of a meal, but many of the children I have fostered had been used to substituting this type of food for meals before they came into care. Breakfast, often bought from the corner shop and eaten on the way to school, would be a chocolate bar, or a bag of crisps and a can of fizzy drink, while the evening meal would be whatever the child could find in the cupboard, and very likely sugar-laden cereal and a packet of biscuits. Often the only 'proper' meal a child had, therefore, was the free school dinner from Monday to Friday. While this type of eating applies to the minority, many children from good homes are overweight and lack essential vitamins and minerals simply because their diets are too high in processed foods. These are attractively packaged and sold to us through advertising on the television. How many of us as parents have given in to our child's pestering in the supermarket and bought a ridiculously expensive, attractively packaged (sugar-laden) cereal because our child had seen it advertised? I'll admit I have.

Many governments across the world are now so concerned about the poor quality of children's diets that they are funding initiatives to try to change the eating habits of a generation. Not only does a bad diet stunt a child's growth and development, and cause obesity and lethargy; it can also produce behavioural problems. I mentioned this in my book *Happy Kids* (a guide to raising well-behaved and contented children) and received hundreds of emails from parents who, after reading my book, suddenly connected some foods with their child's bad behaviour. More of that later, but first let's look at the foods that should be limited in a child's diet:

| Foods | Reason for limiting |
| --- | --- |
| Sweets, biscuits, cakes, ice cream and puddings | High in calories, sugar, fat and artificial additives, low in nutrients |
| Sugary cereal, crisps and processed snack food | High in salt, sugar and artificial additives, low in nutrients |
| Fizzy drinks and squashes | No nutrients, high in sugar and artificial additives |

| Foods | Reason for limiting |
| --- | --- |
| Chips, burgers, sausages, pizza, 'takeaways' and 'fast food' | Very high in fat and calories |
| Ketchups, jam and other sugary spreads | Very high in sugar |

You will probably think of others. Generally speaking, if food is heavily processed and not fresh it is likely to be high in calories, sugar, fat, salt and artificial additives and should be limited. Fortunately ingredients now have to be listed on the food packaging, so check if you are unsure. And remember the ingredients are listed in descending order of the amount included – with the highest first – so if the first ingredient listed is sugar, as with most sweets, then sugar is what that food contains most of. But also remember that a good diet for kids is about limiting these foods, not banning them completely.

## Diet and behaviour

'We are what we eat' is a well-known phrase, meaning the food that goes into our mouths is absorbed by our bodies and therefore becomes part of us. This is especially true for children, who are still growing and use a larger proportion of their food for growth, as well as cell repair and general health, than adults do. But it isn't only the child's body and physical health that are at the mercy of what the child consumes, but also the child's brain and central nervous system. A finely tuned endocrine and hormone system is responsible for mood, behaviour and mental health, and this relies on a well-balanced diet to function efficiently. There is now a wealth of scientific information – from studies and research – that shows that children's (and adult's behaviour) is greatly affected by diet. A healthy diet is therefore essential for both children's physical development and their emotional and mental well-being.

## Sugar

Apart from obvious sugar-laden foods – sweets, biscuits, cakes and puddings, etc. – sugar is added to many other processed foods: for example, baked beans, soups and even some bread. As a result our children have become a nation of 'sweet tooths'. As well as having detrimental long-term physical effects – tooth decay, obesity, diabetes, high blood pressure, etc. – too much sugar can have an immediate effect on mood and behaviour. Most parents have observed the 'high' that too many sweet foods or sugary drinks can have on their child – even the average child without a hyperactivity disorder. The reason for this is that as sugar enters the bloodstream it gives a surge of energy, so the child rushes around on a high; but after the 'sugar rush' comes a low as the body dispenses insulin to stabilize itself. The child then becomes tired, irritable and even aggressive, with a craving for something sweet. So begins a pattern of sugar-related highs and lows, and if the child is prone to mood swings or hyperactivity, refined sugar will fuel it. Sugar intake should therefore be moderated and ideally from a natural source, for example, fruit or honey.

## Caffeine

Although it is unlikely you will give your child a cup of strong black coffee, the equivalent amount of caffeine can be found in a can of many a fizzy drink, added by the manufacturers. Caffeine is a powerful stimulant – which is why many adults drink coffee in the morning to wake them up. Caffeine acts immediately on the central nervous system, giving a powerful but short-lived high. Some bottles and cans of fizzy drink now state that they are 'caffeine free', but they are still in the minority, and you will need to check the label to see if caffeine is present, and in what quantity.

Children's sensitivity to caffeine varies, but studies have shown that even children who are not prone to ADHD (Attention Deficit and Hyperactivity Disorder) can become hyperactive, lose concentration, suffer from insomnia and have challenging behaviour when they drink caffeine-laden fizzy drinks. Caffeine is also addictive, and many children are addicted (from regularly consuming fizzy drinks) without their parents realizing it. The child craves and seeks out the drinks, and suffers the effects of withdrawal – headaches, listlessness, irritability – until they have had their daily 'fix'. Caffeine is best avoided by all parents for their children, and if your child has behavioural problems, particularly ADHD, it is absolutely essential to avoid it. There are plenty of enticing soft drinks and juice alternatives available that don't have added caffeine.

## Food additives

Any chemical that is added to food or drink is given an E number. E-numbered chemicals are added for many reasons, including appearance, shelf life, texture and taste. All food additives, including those with E numbers, must be listed on the label of the food package, but only European countries have adopted the E number classification. Although each chemical additive is tested and has to pass health and safety checks before being allowed into food, what isn't tested is the combination of chemicals, and how this combination reacts in the food or the body. Most processed food and drink contains more than one additive, with a packet of brightly coloured sweets containing upward of ten. Even an innocent-looking yoghurt can contain five or more additives if it is sweetened or made to look like the colour of a particular fruit.

Not all additives are synthetic or have harmful effects, and some have been used for years. Many children suffer no ill effects from eating additive-laden processed food, although cause and effect may not be recognized. While you may spot a link between the stomach ache or sickness your child develops after eating a specific food, a headache after eating a doughnut with bright pink icing, for example, may be missed. The full- and long-term effects of consuming additives are not known and research is ongoing. But there is enough evidence to show that as well as some children experiencing physical reactions to additives, mood, behaviour, learning, energy levels and concentration can be affected. Here is a list of additives that research has shown can cause problems in behaviour, but the list is by no means complete:

| Additive | Possible effects | Food it can be found in |
| --- | --- | --- |
| **E110 Sunset yellow** Allowed in the UK, but banned in Norway | Can cause or aggravate ADHD (Attention Deficit and Hyperactivity Disorder) | Orange squash, orange jelly, marzipan, Swiss roll, apricot jam, citrus marmalade, lemon curd, sweets, hot chocolate mix, packet soups, breadcrumbs, cheese sauce, ice cream, canned fish and some medicines |
| **E104 Quinoline yellow** Allowed in the UK, but banned in Australia, Japan, Norway and the United States | Linked to ADHD, restlessness and irritability | Scotch eggs, smoked haddock, hair products, colognes and a wide range of medications |
| **E122 Carmoisine** Allowed in the UK, but banned in Japan, Norway, Sweden and the United States | Linked to ADHD, sleeplessness and loss of concentration | Blancmange, marzipan, Swiss roll, jams and preserves, sweets, brown sauce, flavoured yoghurts, packet soups, jellies, breadcrumbs and cheesecake mixes |
| **E129 Allura Red** Not allowed in food and drink for children under three; banned in Denmark, Belgium, France, Germany, Switzerland, Sweden, Austria and Norway | Can cause or aggravate ADHD and is linked to irritability and lack of concentration | Sweets, drinks, sauces, medications (and cosmetics) |

| Additive | Possible effects | Food it can be found in |
|---|---|---|
| **E102 Tartrazine** Widely used in the UK, but banned in Norway and Austria | Many children are allergic to it and it has been shown to cause and aggravate ADHD. and Oppositional Defiance Disorder | Fruit squash, fruit cordial, coloured fizzy drinks, instant puddings, cake mixes, custard powder, soups, sauces, ice cream, ice lollies, sweets, chewing gum, marzipan, jam, jelly, marmalade, mustard, yoghurt and many convenience foods |
| **E124 Ponceau 4R** Allowed in the UK, but banned in Norway and the United States | Linked to ADHD and sleep disturbance | Dessert toppings, jelly, salami, seafood dressings, tinned strawberries, fruit pie fillings, cake mixes, cheesecakes, soups and trifles |

If you know or suspect your child is sensitive to certain food additives, then it is obviously advisable to avoid food and drinks that contain them.

# CHAPTER TWO

# What is a good diet for kids?

We all accept that a healthy, well-balanced diet is essential for our child's physical and mental well-being, but what exactly is a well-balanced diet and which foods are best and why? Children need protein, carbohydrates, vitamins and some fat in their diet just as adults do, but they need them in different quantities: more of that later. The best way to make sure your child receives a good diet is to provide a variety of foods, using fresh unprocessed food wherever possible, and limiting foods high in fat and refined sugar. So what exactly does a child need?

## Calories

A calorie is a unit of energy, and the calories in food provide the fuel our bodies need in order to work. Without them our hearts wouldn't beat, our legs and arms wouldn't move and our brains would stop working. The body takes the calories it needs from the food we eat and stores any extra as fat, so that if we eat too many calories we put on weight and if we eat too few we lose weight. A child's calorie requirement is different to adults' and depends on their age, size and how active they are. Children who are going through a growth spurt need to increase their calorie intake, and boys usually need more than girls because they have bigger frames. Now follows a general guideline to the number of calories your child will need, but it is general – based on averages. In the first six months a baby will obtain most, if not all, of its calories from milk.

| Age | Average amount of calories required per day | |
| --- | --- | --- |
| | Boys | Girls |
| Birth–6 months | 700 | 550 |
| 7–12 months | 900 | 800 |
| 1–3 years | 1,200 | 1,160 |
| 4–6 years | 1,700 | 1,540 |
| 7–10 years | 1,970 | 1,740 |
| 11–14 years | 2,220 | 1,845 |
| 15–18 years | 2,755 | 2,110 |

Everything we eat or drink, except water, contains calories. Most packaged food shows the number of calories the food contains on the label. No child should ever be calorie counting; it is the parent's or carer's responsibility to ensure their child receives a good diet, which will include sufficient calories for growth and development but not so many that the child becomes obese. Clearly I haven't the space here to list the calorific content of all foods but here is the amount of calories in some of the foods popular with children.

## Amount of calories in an average serving or the quantity stated

### Cereal with semi-skimmed milk and sugar:

| | | | |
|---|---|---|---|
| Cornflakes | 270 | Crunchy nut cornflakes | 280 |
| Porridge | 260 | Rice Krispies | 270 |
| Shredded Wheat | 240 | Wheat biscuits | 220 |

### Bread, biscuits and cake:

| | | | |
|---|---|---|---|
| Slice of white bread | 85 | Slice of brown bread | 80 |
| Toast with butter and jam | 160 | Plain biscuit | 60 |
| Chocolate biscuit | 85 | Kit Kat | 106 |
| Danish pastry | 287 | Jam doughnut | 140 |
| Jaffa Cake | 46 | Chocolate cake | 300 |

### Fruit:

| | | | |
|---|---|---|---|
| Apple | 50 | Banana | 140 |
| Pear | 70 | Orange | 60 |

### Fast food:

| | | | |
|---|---|---|---|
| Big Mac | 490 | Hamburger | 250 |
| Cheeseburger | 370 | Quarter pounder | 500 |
| Kentucky Fried Chicken | 195 | Fries/chips | 250 |
| Slice of pizza | 170 | | |

### Sweets, chocolate and crisps:

| | | | |
|---|---|---|---|
| Mars bar | 290 | Chocolate ice cream | 160 |
| Milky Way | 117 | Popcorn | 405 |
| Twix | 300 | Snickers | 320 |
| Packet of plain crisps | 130 | Packet of flavoured crisps | 180 |

### Chicken, meat and fish:

| | | | |
|---|---|---|---|
| Chicken breast | 340 | Pork sausage | 75 |
| Beef sausage | 150 | Kebab | 400 |
| Slice of bacon | 65 | Slice of ham | 35 |
| Pork chop | 75 | Lamb chop | 70 |
| 1 chicken dipper | 44 | 1 fish finger | 50 |
| Cod in batter | 420 | Cottage pie | 400 |
| Lasagne | 450 | Spaghetti bolognese | 400 |

### Vegetables:

| | | | |
|---|---|---|---|
| Jacket potato | 100 | Jacket potato with topping | 400 |
| Mashed potatoes | 160 | Baked beans | 120 |
| Peas | 55 | Sweetcorn | 70 |
| Broccoli | 9 | Carrots | 17 |

### Eggs and dairy produce:

| | | | |
|---|---|---|---|
| Portion of butter | 35 | Cheddar cheese 28g | 114 |
| 1 egg | 80 | Plain yoghurt | 60 |
| Fruit yoghurt | 110 | | |

### Drinks:

| | | | |
|---|---|---|---|
| Water | 0 | Cup of semi-skimmed milk, 240ml | 120 |
| Kids' milk shake (semi-skimmed) | 150 | Can of Coca-Cola | 200 |
| Glass of juice | 80 | | |

# Ideal weight

Height and weight charts have largely been replaced by BMI (Body Mass Index) as a way to calculate the correct weight for a child (and adult). However, the calculators can sometimes be complicated to use and the results difficult to interpret, so now follows a general guideline on what your child should weigh at a given height. Remember the heights are averages, so your child will very likely be slightly above or below.

**Average height and weight of boys**

| Age | Height (cm) | Weight (kg) |
| --- | --- | --- |
| Birth | 50.5 | 3.3 |
| 3 months | 61.1 | 6.0 |
| 6 months | 67.8 | 7.8 |
| 9 months | 72.3 | 9.2 |
| 1 year | 76.1 | 10.2 |
| 2 years | 85.6 | 12.3 |
| 3 years | 94.9 | 14.6 |
| 4 years | 102.9 | 16.7 |
| 5 years | 109.9 | 18.7 |
| 6 years | 116.1 | 20.7 |
| 7 years | 121.7 | 22.9 |
| 8 years | 127.0 | 25.3 |
| 9 years | 132.2 | 28.1 |
| 10 years | 137.5 | 31.4 |
| 11 years | 140.0 | 32.2 |
| 12 years | 147.0 | 37.0 |
| 13 years | 153.0 | 40.9 |
| 14 years | 160.0 | 47.0 |
| 15 years | 166.0 | 52.6 |
| 16 years | 171.0 | 58.0 |
| 17 years | 175.0 | 62.7 |
| 18 years | 177.0 | 65.0 |

## Average height and weight of girls

| Ages | Height (cm) | Weight (kg) |
|---|---|---|
| Birth | 49.9 | 3.2 |
| 3 months | 60.2 | 5.4 |
| 6 months | 66.6 | 7.2 |
| 9 months | 71.1 | 8.6 |
| 1 year | 75.0 | 9.5 |
| 2 years | 84.5 | 11.8 |
| 3 years | 93.9 | 14.1 |
| 4 years | 101.6 | 16.0 |
| 5 years | 108.4 | 17.7 |
| 6 years | 114.6 | 19.5 |
| 7 years | 120.6 | 21.8 |
| 8 years | 126.4 | 24.8 |
| 9 years | 132.2 | 28.5 |
| 10 years | 138.3 | 32.5 |
| 11 years | 142.0 | 33.7 |
| 12 years | 148.0 | 38.7 |
| 13 years | 150.0 | 44.0 |
| 14 years | 155.0 | 48.0 |
| 15 years | 161.0 | 51.5 |
| 16 years | 162.0 | 53.0 |
| 17 years | 163.0 | 54.0 |
| 18 years | 164.0 | 54.4 |

# Protein

Protein is another essential requirement in a child's diet. Protein is the building block of life. Every cell in the human body contains protein, and protein is needed for growth and repair.

**A child's daily requirement of protein**

| Age and sex | Grams of protein recommended per day |
| --- | --- |
| 1–3 years, girls and boys | 13 |
| 4–8 years, girls and boys | 19 |
| 9–13 years, girls and boys | 34 |
| 14–18, girls | 46 |
| 14–18, boys | 52 |

Most food that is packaged lists the amount of protein per gram the food contains on the label. If protein is not shown, then the food doesn't contain any protein. However, although this information may be helpful, if a child is given a well-balanced, varied diet which includes protein at the main meal they will have enough protein for their needs. Protein is found in many foods, even in small amounts in cake and bread. Foods rich in protein should be included daily in a child's diet and these are:

* meat, poultry, fish, shellfish and eggs
* beans, pulses, nuts, grains and seeds
* milk and milk products
* soya products and vegetable protein foods

Some typical values of protein-rich food are:

**Grams of protein per 100g or the quantity stated**

| | | | |
|---|---|---|---|
| Cup of semi-skimmed milk (240ml) | 8 | Yoghurt | 4.5 |
| | | 1 medium egg | 6 |
| Lean chicken | 30 | Lean meat | 30 |
| Nuts | 21 | Bacon | 16 |
| Baked beans | 10 | 1 banana | 1 |
| Slice of bread | 3 | Cheddar cheese | 30 |
| Fish | 16 | Pasta | 12 |
| 1 teaspoon peanut butter | 4 | Peas | 6 |
| Pizza | 12 | Porridge | 12 |
| Potatoes | 20 | Rice | 7 |
| Sausages | 14 | Spinach | 3 |
| 1 teaspoon yeast extract (Marmite) | 3 | | |

## Carbohydrates

The carbohydrates our bodies take from the food we eat are our main source of energy. The more active a child is the more carbohydrate he or she will need. Carbohydrates also have the function of setting protein to work – for growth and repair – which is why the two food groups are eaten together: meat and potatoes, bread and cheese, etc. There are two types of carbohydrate – complex and simple – and the body needs both of them:

**Complex carbohydrates** are found in fresh and processed foods and are sometimes called starchy foods. Foods providing complex carbohydrates include: bananas, beans, brown rice, chickpeas, lentils, nuts, oats, parsnips, potatoes, root vegetables, sweetcorn, wholegrain cereals, wholemeal bread, wholemeal cereals, wholemeal flour, wholemeal pasta, and are considered 'good' carbs. Refined starches are also complex carbohydrates but are not so good because the refining process removes nutrients from the food and concentrates the sugar. They are found in: biscuits, pastries and cakes, pizzas, sugary breakfast cereals, white bread, white flour, white pasta, white rice.

**Simple carbohydrates** are also known as sugars – natural and refined. Natural sugars are found in fruit and vegetables. Refined sugars are in: biscuits, cakes, pastries, chocolate, honey, jams, jellies, sugar, pizzas, processed foods and sauces, soft drinks, sweets, snack bars.

Children over two should have a diet where approximately half their calories come from carbohydrates, and preferably from 'good' sources, so the amount of refined sugar and starch – from cakes and biscuits, etc. – is limited. But there is no need to carb count. If your child is eating a variety of foods in well-balanced meals they will be eating the carbohydrates their body needs.

## Fibre

Fibre is another important component in a healthy, balanced diet and many children don't eat enough fibre. We obtain fibre from plant-based foods: for example, fruit, vegetables, wholemeal bread and pasta, and some cereals. Not only is fibre good for the digestive system (it prevents constipation), but it is also good for the heart and for blood circulation, and lowers cholesterol and blood sugar levels, so preventing diabetes in later life. Fibre provides bulk to a diet, so any child on a weight-reduction programme would be advised to eat a high-fibre diet, which will make them feel full and therefore control hunger and appetite.

The amount of fibre a child needs in their diet is shown below. It will also be listed on most packaged foods. Fibre in the form of bran can be added to a child's diet but if a child is eating plenty of natural wholesome foods they should be getting the fibre they need. Problems arise if a child consistently eats a diet high in processed food, which contains little or no fibre.

## A child's daily requirement of fibre

| Age and sex of child | Amount of fibre required per day in grams |
|---|---|
| 1–3 years, girls and boys | 19 |
| 4–8 years, girls and boys | 25 |
| 9–13 years, girls | 26 |
| 9–13 years, boys | 31 |
| 14–18 years, girls | 26 |
| 14–18 years, boys | 38 |

## Good sources of fibre

| Food | Average portion size | Grams of fibre |
|---|---|---|
| Vegetables: | | |
| Baked beans | 200g | 7.4 |
| Broccoli | 85g | 2 |
| Carrots | 60g | 1.5 |

| Frozen mixed veg | 90g | 4 |
| Green beans | 90g | 1.7 |
| Peas | 90g | 4.6 |
| Potato | 1 medium | 4.5 |
| Sweetcorn | 90g | 1.3 |
| Vegetable soup | 1 bowl (200ml) | 1.5 |

### Fruit:

| | | |
| --- | --- | --- |
| Apple (with skin) | 1 medium | 3 |
| Banana | 1 medium | 3 |
| Blackberries | 50g | 4 |
| Orange | 1 medium | 3 |
| Pear | 1 medium | 5 |
| Raspberries | 50g | 4 |

### Cereals, breads, grains:

| | | |
| --- | --- | --- |
| Brown rice, cooked | 100g | 1 |
| Wholemeal bread | 1 slice | 2.2 |
| Bagel | 1 | 1.4 |
| Wholemeal pasta, cooked | 200g | 7 |
| All-Bran | 4 tablespoons | 8 |
| Shredded Wheat | 2 | 5.5 |
| Porridge | 1 bowl (200g) | 2 |
| Mixed nuts | 50g | 3 |

So that if, for example, a child aged eight has two Shredded Wheat for breakfast, sandwiches made from three or four slices of wholemeal bread and a piece of fruit for lunch, and an evening meal of meat and two veg, they will have had their daily requirement of fibre. However, if the same child skips breakfast or has a couple of biscuits, a white bread sandwich and a packet of crisps for lunch, and pasta and cake for the evening meal, their diet will be lacking in fibre, which causes constipation. A general rule is that if the food is plant based then it will have a high fibre content and should be included in a child's daily diet.

## Fat

Fat in children's (and adults') diets has had a lot of bad press recently because in the Western world we often eat too much fat. However, fat is an essential component of a well-balanced diet and performs a number of functions:

* Fat is a good source of energy. 1 gram provides 9 calories, which is more than double the calories in protein or carbohydrate.
* Fat transports vitamins A, D, E and K around the body, supplying the body with essential nutrients.
* Fat often makes food taste better.
* Fat is a source of fatty acids (EFAs), which are thought to have a positive effect on the heart and immune system.
* Fat stored in the body protects internal organs as well as being a fuel reserve. Should a child fall sick and not eat properly the body burns the fat for the calories it needs, which is why we can lose weight if we are ill.

Saturated fat is found in lard, butter, hard margarine, cheese, whole milk and anything containing these ingredients, such as cakes, biscuits, pies and chocolate; it is also in the white fat on meat and the skin on poultry. Unsaturated fat comes from vege-table sources and is usually considered a healthier alternative to saturated fat. It is found in sunflower, soya and olive oils, soft margarine and oily fish – for example, mackerel, sardines and salmon. Cod liver oil can be given as a supplement to children and some research suggests it is beneficial to do so.

The amount of fat a child needs is usually considered as a percentage of their daily calorific requirement and it is quite high. See the table below.

**A child's daily requirement of fat**

| Age | Required percentage of calories coming from fat |
| --- | --- |
| 1 year | 30–40 per cent |
| 2–3 years | 30–35 per cent |
| 4–18 years | 25–35 per cent |

Generally vegetables, fruit (apart from avocados), white fish, grains and cereal contain little or no fat. Examples of good sources of fat are listed below.

**Good sources of fat**

| Food | Portion size | Calories | % fat |
| --- | --- | --- | --- |
| Dairy produce: | | | |
| Butter | 1 teaspoon | 80 | 99 |
| Cheddar cheese | 50g | 200 | 70 |
| Whole milk | 150ml | 100 | 55 |
| Egg | 1 large | 80 | 60 |
| Yoghurt, whole milk | 100g | 62 | 50 |

## Meat:

| | | | |
|---|---|---|---|
| Bacon | 2 rashers | 70 | 70 |
| Beef | 50g | 150 | 40 |
| Mince | 50g | 160 | 60 |
| Sausage | 1 medium | 150 | 70 |
| Lamb | 50g | 140 | 60 |
| Ham | 1 medium slice | 40 | 65 |
| Chicken breast (without skin) | 50g | 80 | 20 |
| Chicken drumstick | 1 small | 80 | 70 |

## Nuts:

| | | | |
|---|---|---|---|
| Almonds | 5 | 35 | 30 |
| Cashews | 5 | 45 | 70 |
| Peanuts | 50g | 300 | 70 |
| Peanut butter | 1 teaspoon | 100 | 80 |

Remember that fat is an essential part of your child's diet, but if your child is regularly eating too much fat and you are looking to reduce the amount of fat in his or her diet, then try the following:

* Limit cakes, biscuits and savoury snacks, which are high in fat.
* Trim fat off meat and skin off poultry.
* Grill, poach, steam, bake or microwave rather than fry foods.
* Swap whole milk for semi-skimmed.
* Choose low-fat dairy products.
* Use vegetable oil and low-fat spreads rather than lard, butter or hard margarine.

# Vitamins and minerals

Vitamins and minerals are needed by the body for growth, repair and staying healthy. They are taken from the food we eat and absorbed by the body. Each vitamin and mineral has a specific role and should be eaten daily, as most vitamins and minerals cannot be stored by the body. For daily requirement, function and foods where the vitamins and minerals are found, see the table below.

| Vitamin or mineral | Function in body | Age in years and RDA | Food source |
|---|---|---|---|
| Vitamin A | Promotes healthy eyes, skin, bone and cell growth; boosts immune system | 1–3: 300mg<br>4–8: 400mg<br>9–13: 600mg<br>14–16: 700mg F, 900mg M | Milk, eggs, cheese, liver, dark green and deep yellow fruit and vegetables – e.g. carrots, spinach, apricots |
| Vitamin B complex | Promotes growth, red blood cells, nerve function, energy, muscles, hormones, immune system | B vitamins are only needed in small amounts | Dairy products, poultry, fish, eggs, meat, wholegrains, cereals, beans, peas, nuts, green vegetables |

| Vitamin or mineral | Function in body | Age in years and RDA | Food source |
|---|---|---|---|
| Vitamin C | Fights disease; heals wounds; promotes growth, brain function, healthy bones, | 1–3: 15mg<br>4–8: 25mg<br>9–13: 45mg<br>14–18: 65mg F, 75mg M<br><br>teeth and gums | Fruit and vegetables, especially oranges, tomatoes, peppers, strawberries broccoli, spinach |
| Vitamin D | Works with calcium for strong bones and teeth; maintains nervous system | Only a little is needed and the body can store it | Eggs, milk, oily fish, sunlight |
| Iron | Transports oxygen around the body in red blood cells | 1–3: 7mg<br>4–8: 10mg<br>9–13: 8mg<br>14–18: 15mg F, 11mg M | Green vegetables, meat, poultry, fish, beans, lentils, soy products, fortified cereals |
| Calcium | Builds strong bones and teeth | 1–3: 500mg<br>4–8: 800mg<br>9–13: 1000mg<br>14–18: 1300mg | Milk, cheese, yoghurt, dark green vegetables, soy, and fortified products |

| Vitamin or mineral | Function in body | Age in years and RDA | Food source |
| --- | --- | --- | --- |
| Magnesium | Helps building of bones and teeth, muscle functioning, nervous system, immune system, hearing and blood sugar levels | 1–3: 80mg<br>4–8: 130mg<br>9–13: 240mg<br>14–18: 360mg F, 410mg M | Wholegrains, cereals, nuts, seeds, beans, bananas, dairy products, green leafy vegetables, meat, seafood |
| Zinc | Promotes growth, wound healing, healthy skin and energy production; supports immune system | 1–3: 3mg<br>4–8: 5mg<br>9–13: 8mg<br>14–18: 9mg F, 11mg M | Red meat, poultry, nuts, fortified cereals, seafood, dairy and soy products, yeast, legumes (dried beans and peas) |

RDA = recommended daily allowance; mg = micrograms; F = female, M = male

Although vitamins and minerals are just as important to the body as calories, and protein, carbohydrates and fat, we only need them in small amounts. As with all nutrients, if your child is eating a well-balanced diet that includes fresh fruit and vegetables they will have the daily intake of vitamins and minerals that are essential for growth, development and maintaining a healthy body and mind.

# Fluid

Notice I haven't said water, because fluid can be obtained from many different sources including soups, fruit juices, milk, vegetables and fruit – tomatoes, grapes, melons and oranges, for example, are 90 per cent water. It is vital a child has sufficient fluid intake, as much as it is that a child eats. The human body is 63 per cent water and the brain 77 per cent. Drinking regularly, and so keeping the body and brain hydrated, is therefore essential for body and brain to function in a child or adult. By the time a child is saying they are thirsty they are already dehydrated, and even mild dehydration can cause headaches, tiredness, loss of concentration and irritability.

Salt is added to most snacks and processed food and salt is a diuretic: that is, it makes you wee more, which results in dehydration if the lost fluid is not replaced. Children are more prone to dehydration than adults, as a result of diet (such as salty snacks) and activity (fluid is lost in sweat), and because they can forget to drink. Also, the school routine doesn't always offer enough opportunity for children to drink during the day.

Trials have shown that if children take a bottle of water into school, and are encouraged to drink at regular intervals during the day, there isn't the dip in concentration and learning that is often experienced in late morning and afternoon. The ideal drink for children is water, but if your child really won't drink water, then lightly lace it with additive-free squash or fruit juice. Your child should be drinking regularly throughout the day, and apart from the fluid obtained from soups and fruit, etc., he or she should drink 1.5–2 litres a day, or more if they are very active or the weather is hot.

# CHAPTER THREE

# Meals and eating

It is important your child eats and drinks regularly throughout the day and the best way of ensuring this happens is to establish regular mealtimes. Not only will this encourage your child to eat in a calm and enjoyable manner but family mealtimes are also a sociable event, where family members meet and talk amicably in a friendly and supportive atmosphere. Many children who come into foster care have never had mealtimes or sat at a dining table and do not know how to use a knife and fork. One of the first things I do when a child arrives is to establish a routine, which includes regular bath and bed times, and meals at set times at which the family eats at the table. A routine where all members of the family know what is expected feels safe, secure and reliable to a child, and so too with mealtimes.

## The importance of mealtimes

* The child's food and fluid intake can be easily monitored by the parent to ensure the child is eating a healthy diet, which is sufficient for their needs but not excessive. It will be obvious what the child has eaten from what remains on the plate.

* Family meals at the table encourage family members to bond with each other and enjoy each other's company.
* Children can learn table manners and how to use cutlery, usually by imitating their parents. Table manners and knowing how to use cutlery are very important in adult life.
* Children can sit upright at a table (rather than slouching on a sofa), which encourages good digestion.

So these are the main reasons why children should eat family meals at the table, but what exactly is a good mealtime and how do we achieve it?

## Establishing good mealtimes

* Aim to have at least one family meal together every day that includes all family members. For practical reasons this is often the evening meal.
* Establish good hygiene, with the children washing their hands before the meal and changing out of any very dirty clothes, for example if they have just come in from the garden caked in mud.
* Create good practice by calling the family for dinner a couple of minutes before the food is ready, so that they arrive at the table just before you serve the meal.
* As far as is practical, include children in the preparation of the meal, laying the table and clearing away afterwards. Children love to help and even young children can be taught to lay a place at a table.

* Switch off the television during mealtimes so that the focus is on the meal, the people and eating, not on the television screen. Likewise, books, magazines and hand-held game consoles should be left away from the table.

* Provide nutritious food that is simple, varied and appealing to children. While an adult might relish Stilton and broccoli soup, followed by glazed duck breast with port and caramelized orange sauce, most children will not.

* Serve the same food to all family members unless your child has special dietary needs. I deal with food fussiness on the next page.

* Keep the talk at the table light and positive, so that all family members have a chance to share their news as well as eating. The meal table is not a place for siblings to continue a disagreement or for parents to criticize or discipline their children.

* As far as possible have meals at the same time each day. This will ensure children (and adults) eat and drink regularly, which is essential to maintain energy levels and concentration.

* Start young. As soon as your child can comfortably sit upright – between four and six months – bring them to the table in a high chair. If good eating habits are established early, your child will continue to have them throughout their lives.

# Food fussiness and refusal to eat

Nothing is guaranteed to wind up a parent and worry them more than a child picking at their food or refusing to eat. As parents we nurture and love our children and take pride in seeing them grow and thrive. Food is essential to sustain life and therefore an intrinsic part of that nurturing and love, so that if a child rejects the food we have lovingly prepared then it is easy to feel they are rejecting us. Children soon realize how much it means to us as parents to see our child eat healthily – look how much trouble we go to buying and preparing food – so accepting or rejecting food can be used by a child as a way of controlling a parent. I say more on that below.

The majority of children I've fostered have come to me with some form of 'eating disorder': refusing to eat, eating the smallest of amounts, eating only sweet foods, or gorging or bingeing until they are physically sick. However, all the children, without exception, significantly improved or recovered completely, and were eating healthily by the time they left me. My adopted daughter, Lucy, overcame anorexia within a year of coming to me. Based on training, research and twenty-five years of fostering experience, here are my guidelines for achieving healthy eating.

**Expect your child to eat** As you should expect good behaviour from your child (see *Happy Kids*), so you should expect your child to eat – at the table and the same food as other family members. Be confident in your expectation and don't falter. Your child will soon realize that eating as everyone else in the family is doing is the norm and your expectations will be complied with.

**Make healthy eating the norm** You and the other members of your family need to make sure healthy eating at mealtimes is the norm by setting a good example. You can't expect your child to eat heartily, healthily and happily if you are sitting there picking at your food, claiming you are on a diet or not eating at all.

**Start early** Establish good eating practices for your child as soon as you can, ideally when he or she can sit upright and join the family at the table. If good eating practices are established early in childhood, a child is far less likely to develop eating difficulties later. If your child is already a problem eater, start the new routine (see above) as soon as possible and be firm with your expectations.

**Encourage children to feed themselves** Give your child responsibility for feeding themselves as soon as they are able. Children can start eating finger foods from six months, and they can also be encouraged to hold the spoon, bottle or feeder cup while you feed them. Feeding him- or herself is one of the many self-care skills a child needs to be taught early. It gives the child confidence and autonomy, and a child is far less likely to reject food if they are feeding themselves rather than having food pushed into their mouth.

**Check nothing is worrying your child** If your child suddenly starts to refuse food, make sure there is nothing worrying them. Worries can take away a child's appetite just as they can an adult's. Don't ask the child at the table if they are worried about anything, but wait until later when there are just the two of you and you have time. You may need to coax the worry out of your child, so be relaxed, gentle, and take your time. If there is something worrying your child, reassure them and deal with the problem.

**Give children equal amounts of attention** Make sure your child is receiving their fair share of attention – both at the meal table and generally. If your child is feeling left out or undervalued for any reason, refusing food can be a good way of getting attention, just as naughty behaviour can. Food and emotion are linked, and extreme eating disorders such as anorexia or bulimia have emotional/psychological roots, which is why in such cases the whole family goes into therapy and not just the sufferer.

**Serve suitable-sized portions** Make sure you are not giving your child too much food. Children's stomachs are a lot smaller than adults', so they feel full sooner. If you give your child more food then they can eat they will of course leave some. A general guideline is that a child's stomach is the size of their fist, as is an adult's. Give your child a suitable-sized portion; they can always have seconds if they are still hungry.

**Keep meals simple** Keep food simple, especially with young children. If a child has too many different foods on their plate (or too much), they may take the easiest solution and eat nothing.

**Limit snacking** While a little snack mid-morning or mid-afternoon will sustain a child's energy levels between meals, too many, too large or very sweet snacks will dramatically reduce a child's appetite at the meal table.

**Never use food for punishment** Never use the withholding of food as a means of punishment: *You'll go to your room without any tea.* Apart from food deprivation being unacceptable, you will also be storing up trouble for later by bringing food into the emotional arena, so the next time your child is angry with you they will refuse to eat. And try not to bribe children with sweet things, tempting though it can be at times: *When you've done your reading/homework/piano practice you can have a chocolate bar.* Use something unconnected with food as a reward – for example, extra television time, or another fifteen minutes' playing outside before bedtime. Linking food and behaviour will cause problems.

**Be firm** Lots of books talk about presenting food and then taking it away if the child doesn't eat. I doubt many parents could do this. I don't adhere to this philosophy. In my experience a parent (or carer) often has to be firm with a child if they are completely refusing to eat or not eating enough for their needs. If necessary, allow your child extra time to eat. Chat lightly and allow other siblings to leave the table if they have long ago finished while you remain or busy yourself nearby. You don't want your child to feel isolated by being left alone at the table, but neither should they force siblings to sit at the table. Don't point out the child's slow eating, although you can say lightly: *Come on, finish your meal and then you can play* (or whatever they are planning to do after the meal). If necessary, tell them they have to eat so much before they can leave the table. The longer a child is allowed to indulge in poor eating, the bigger the problem will be to solve, so be firm.

**Accept genuine dislikes** Obviously don't force your child to eat a food he or she genuinely doesn't like. All children have food preferences and a few dislikes are acceptable, but refusing to eat all nutritious food is not.

**Don't allow food to be a means of control** Food refusal, as already mentioned, can be a way of controlling or blackmailing a parent. Don't pander to a child's fussy ways and don't be tempted to give them something different if they have eaten little or nothing. You will find that a child who is using food as a way to control and manipulate you will like something one day and reject it another. If you give the child something different (at the meal table or later) it will prove to the child that he or she has status above the rest of the family and is in control.

**Use common sense** Don't worry if your child doesn't want to eat one day or eats very little. A child's body usually regulates its food intake and that can vary from day to day. If a child is physically active one day they will need more than if they have been travelling in a car or sitting on a sofa. Or possibly they may be sickening for something: sometimes a child suddenly refusing to eat is the first indication they are not well. If your child refuses food, don't react; just assume it will pass and the child will be eating normally in the morning and in most cases that is what will happen. If not, assess the situation, include the child in mealtimes and follow the above guidelines.

CHAPTER FOUR

# Breakfast

Breakfast is often said to be the most important meal of the day and for very good reason. The word 'breakfast' means to break a fast – that is, to end a long period without food or drink. Most children will have slept between eight and twelve hours. During that time their bodies will have been dormant and not have taken in food or fluid. On waking, their energy and fluid levels will be low, just as adults' will be, so eating and drinking first thing in the morning is essential to rehydrate the body and boost energy levels.

Studies have shown that children who regularly eat breakfast are generally healthier, concentrate better at school, perform better at tests, participate more in physical activities and are less likely to be overweight than children who don't eat breakfast. Children who skip breakfast often feel tired and irritable by mid-morning as their blood sugar and fluid levels plummet, resulting in lack of concentration, restlessness and lethargy. It is far too long for a child to go without eating from dinner one evening – usually eaten between six o'clock and eight o'clock – to lunch the following day – usually eaten around twelve noon: that's between eighteen and twenty hours.

Breakfast is therefore essential for all children, even if it is light, and it must include a drink.

# Breakfast routine

Breakfast in the school/working week may understandably be rushed – the clock is ticking and you and your family need to be out of the door at a set time to go to school and work. Even so, for the reasons given in Chapter Three, breakfast should be treated as a mealtime and therefore eaten at the table or breakfast bar with as many family members present as possible. As with all meals, the atmosphere should be calm and sociable, although the conversation may not be very stimulating first thing in the morning – I know it isn't in my house!

Clearly it is up to you and your partner how you plan your morning routine and whether your children wash and dress before they come down to breakfast or eat in their nightwear and then wash and dress afterwards. Whatever your routine, make sure it allows enough time for your child to eat their breakfast, even if it means getting them up ten minutes earlier. Ten minutes in the morning on a tight time schedule can make a huge difference.

Make sure your morning routine is the same each day, certainly for the school/working week. The weekends are probably more relaxed, with breakfast eaten later and in a more leisurely way. As with all routines, having the same one each morning will ensure your children know what is expected of them: when they have to be downstairs, ready for breakfast, and when they need to leave the house for school. I have a child's clock on the wall in the children's bedrooms and even young children who can't read the time can be taught the basics: that they need to have finished dressing before the big hand points to a certain number. It can be fun – a race against time – and as well as teaching the child the time it builds their confidence by giving them responsibility for coming to breakfast on time. And it's far more pleasant for you than standing at the foot of the stairs yelling to the children to come down now or they'll be late.

## Breakfast food

What children eat for breakfast is important. The food should ideally contain mainly protein and carbohydrate, which will boost their energy levels for longer than high-sugar and high-fat foods. In this chapter I give suggestions for quick breakfasts and ones that require longer preparation below, but a word of warning: some sugary cereals, toaster pastries, breakfast biscuits, cereal and yogurt bars contain no more nutrition than a candy bar, with most of the calories coming from sugar. Check on the packet or wrapper of these items before buying them.

## Drinks for breakfast

It is vital children have a drink at breakfast as otherwise they will quickly become dehydrated. Younger children can have milk, water, fruit juice or drinking chocolate, and older children may enjoy a cup of tea. They should not have any fizzy drinks. Apart from being bad for teeth, these have high levels of sugar and often contain caffeine, both of which will give the child an immediate high, but this will be short-lived, leaving them listless, irritable and dehydrated, as caffeine is a diuretic.

# Quick breakfast ideas that kids love

## Cereal

A bowl of cereal with semi-skimmed milk can be a good start to the day for kids. Avoid high-sugar cereals and choose from wheat flakes, wheat 'biscuits', porridge, muesli or any wholewheat or wholegrain cereal. Check on the packet for the nutritional content of the cereal and always have a packet of cereal in the cupboard for a quick breakfast. Nearly all children are happy to eat cereal, and diced or sliced fruit can easily be added for additional nutrition. If your child only ever eats cereal for breakfast, then rotate the type of cereal he or she has. As well as keeping breakfast interesting, different cereals contain different nutrients and varying the cereal will therefore contribute towards a balanced diet.

## Toast

Toast should ideally be made from wholemeal bread, although don't fret if your child prefers white bread – most children do. Spread the toast with butter or a butter substitute, and then add a topping: cream cheese, yeast extract (Marmite), honey, peanut butter or any topping the child likes. Use high-sugar spreads sparingly – jams, preserves, chocolate spread, for example, are always high in sugar, even when the jar states 'sugar reduced'. A slice of cheese, ham or other cold meat can easily be added to a slice of toast, giving protein and additional calories and nutrients. One child I fostered loved fish paste on his toast in the morning, which although I couldn't stomach made him happy and our cat very excited.

## Bread rolls

To add variety, try bread rolls instead of toast. Although rolls can be eaten cold, they are especially appetizing when warmed in the oven or microwave. I am a great fan of partly baked rolls, which can be bought from the supermarket. They take only a few minutes to cook in a preheated oven, and there's nothing to beat the smell, texture and taste of fresh warm bread first thing in the morning. Cut the baked roll in half and spread with butter or a butter substitute and then add a topping as for toast. If you are adding cheese, ham or other foods, close the roll again to make a crusty roll sandwich, which children love and find easy to eat. Your child might like to add some relish or sauce, and if you can slip in a slice of tomato, cucumber, pepper or other piece of salad, so much the better.

## Bagels

Most children like bagels and they come in different varieties, including plain, seeded, sundried tomato, onion, cinnamon and blueberry. Stand the bagel on its side, cut in half and then lightly toast, or warm in the oven or microwave. Spread and top as for toast, again adding a nutritious filling if desired, such as ham, cheese, salad or even an egg if you have the time to cook one. Obviously choose a topping or filling that complements the type of bagel – savoury with savoury and sweet with sweet. So a slice of ham or cheese will go nicely with a sundried tomato or a seeded bagel, and honey can be spread on a plain bagel, and butter or butter substitute on a cinnamon or blueberry bagel.

## English muffins

These are not cakes as American muffins are but yeast-based dough – that is, a type of bread – and have been popular in England since the eighteenth century. Muffins come in different varieties, including plain, sourdough, cheese, wholegrain and cinnamon. They have a softer texture than toast or bagels and can be bought from most supermarkets and bakers. Prepare the muffin by cutting it in half and toasting or warming as with a roll or bagel. Add a topping that complements the flavour of the muffin and close for easy eating.

## Croissants

These are buttery, flaky pastries, originally associated with France. Children love them. They are easy to eat and you can now buy low-fat croissants. Warm in an oven or microwave. Savoury or sweet fillings can be added, or just spread thinly with butter.

## Fruit

I always include a piece of fresh fruit at breakfast in addition to whatever else the child is eating. It can be added to a bowl of cereal or served separately on a small plate or dish. Make the fruit look appealing and easy to eat by peeling and slicing as necessary. Try half a dozen seedless grapes, half an apple thinly sliced, a small sliced banana, or half an orange or tangerine, peeled and segmented with pith and pips removed. Once fruit is peeled it soon dries out and discolours, so prepare the fruit as the child arrives at the table for breakfast – it only takes a minute or so. Canned fruit can also be used but choose those that contain natural juice rather than heavy syrup, which is in effect sugar. Some children will make a breakfast of fruit, which is fine, but if they do, make sure they have enough protein and carbohydrate at lunch to sustain them through the day.

## Yoghurts

Yoghurts come in many flavours and varieties and are popular with children, as they are easy to eat and often sweetened. They can be added to breakfast or used instead of breakfast if your child won't eat anything more substantial. Check the contents on the carton and avoid any with a high sugar content or with a long list of food additives. Yoghurt is basically fermented milk, so should contain no more than milk, a bacterial culture (used to allow the fermentation) and a little sugar or fruit. Be wary of large amounts of sugar preservatives, colourings, flavourings, sweeteners, gum, stabilizers, emulsifiers and anything else unrelated to milk (remember ingredients are listed in order – highest first). Yoghurt can be introduced into a baby's diet at six months.

## Smoothies

A smoothie is food and a drink and can be a healthy alternative or an addition to a 'solid' breakfast. If time is short in the morning, smoothies can be prepared the night before and left in the fridge. The basis of a smoothie is milk, yoghurt or soy milk, with fruit and a little honey or sugar to taste. All the ingredients go into a blender to produce a smooth thick 'drink'. The consistency of a smoothie will depend on the amount of milk you use, and it can be drunk or eaten with a spoon depending on how thick it is. Smoothies are very nutritious and filling and provide calories, protein, carbohydrates, fat, vitamins and minerals. If you are buying a ready-made smoothie from a supermarket or fast-food restaurant, check the content, as some are very high in sugar and calories and have additives. You can be adventurous when making smoothies and experiment with what you put in to suit your family's tastes. Banana is a good fruit to use, as it gives the smoothie texture, taste and sweetness as well as being packed with carbohydrates and protein for energy. Tinned or frozen fruit can be used instead of fresh, and crushed ice cubes can be added.

Here are a few suggestions to get you started. Put all the ingredients in a blender and blend until smooth. Serve in a glass or dish with a spoon.

*Basic smoothie*

| | |
|---|---|
| 100ml semi-skimmed milk | 100ml plain yoghurt |
| ½ banana, sliced | 1 teaspoon honey or sugar |

Add another fruit:

| | |
|---|---|
| 100ml semi-skimmed milk | 100ml plain yoghurt |
| ½ banana, sliced | 1 teaspoon honey or sugar |
| 4–6 large strawberries | |

Try soy, oats and vanilla for a different taste and texture:

| | |
|---|---|
| 150ml milk or soy milk | 45g rolled oats |
| 1 banana, sliced | 4–6 large strawberries |
| ½ teaspoon vanilla essence | 1 teaspoon honey or sugar |

Try different combinations of fruit:

| | |
|---|---|
| 1 banana, sliced | 50g blueberries or raspberries |
| 100ml orange juice | 1 tablespoon of honey or sugar |

| | |
|---|---|
| 1 peach, sliced | 1 mango, diced |
| 50ml vanilla soy milk | 50ml orange juice |

Try adding crushed ice cubes:

| | |
|---|---|
| 4 large strawberries | 50ml milk |
| 50ml pineapple juice | 50ml vanilla yoghurt |
| 1 teaspoon honey or sugar | 2 ice cubes |

All the suggestions above are nutritious and will give your child a healthy start to the day. They can all be prepared in 5 minutes.

## Cooked breakfasts

Now for some suggestions for children's breakfast when you and your family have more time, for example at the weekends and in school holidays. Cooked breakfasts take a little longer to prepare but they are well worth the effort. In my house cooked breakfast at the weekend has become a family tradition, which we all enjoy. There's nothing like the smell of a cooked breakfast to entice children and teenagers from their beds at the weekends, and with more time children can help prepare the meal and then clear away afterwards. Here are some suggestions that children will find satisfying and are also nutritious. Most take under fifteen minutes to prepare.

## Full English breakfast

The full English breakfast has a worldwide reputation, although what exactly constitutes a full English breakfast is sometimes open to debate. Choose three or more foods from the following and your child will be having not only a cooked English breakfast but also a wholesome, energy-packed and nutritious start to the day.

**Bacon** One or two rashers, fried or grilled.

**Egg** Usually fried, but can be poached, scrambled or boiled and peeled. (For cooking eggs, see page 47.)

**Sausage** Fried or grilled. Choose a meatless sausage if your family is vegetarian.

**Tomato** Usually cut in half and fried, grilled or baked. Tinned tomatoes can also be used.

**Mushrooms** Usually fried, or can be grilled but brush with oil first to prevent drying. Can also be boiled. Always wash before cooking.

**Hash browns** To serve 4, grate 4 medium potatoes into a bowl, add 1 medium onion, grated, 1 beaten egg, salt and pepper. Mix well. Heat a little oil in a frying pan and add spoonfuls of the mixture. Flatten and when cooked until brown on one side, turn and cook on the other. Hash browns can also be bought ready made and frozen from the supermarket, and these can be fried or baked in the oven.

**Black pudding** Some would say that a full English breakfast should include a slice of black pudding. Black pudding is a type of sausage with a high content of dried animal blood. It can be bought from a butcher or delicatessen counter. You either love it or hate it. None of my family are fans but your child may like to try it.

**Toast or fried bread** Usually cut diagonally and served on the same plate as the cooked breakfast, toast or fried bread is essential for mopping up the juices from the egg, baked beans or tomatoes. To make fried bread, heat a little oil in a frying pan and cook both sides of a slice of bread until crispy and golden, which usually takes 2–3 minutes. White bread works better than wholemeal.

**Baked beans** Irresistible when the red sauce mixes with the yellow egg yolk on the plate.

The full English breakfast sometimes receives a bad press, but eaten occasionally and with oil used instead of lard for frying, a cooked breakfast is a satisfying meal that will see your child through to lunchtime. And a cooked breakfast doesn't have to be saved for breakfast but can eaten for lunch, dinner or at any time in the day, as many cafés and restaurants announce on their menus: *the all-day breakfast.*

## Omelette

Beat 2 eggs in a bowl with a pinch of salt and pepper to taste. Heat a little oil or butter in a frying pan and then pour in the egg mixture. After about a minute, when the mixture is setting and half-cooked, add a filling (grated cheese is popular) over half of the omelette. Cook for another minute and then flip the half without the filling over the half with the filling. Cook both sides for another 15–30 seconds until light golden brown. The filling can be anything your child likes: for example, diced cooked meat, sliced and cooked mushrooms, baked beans, sliced tomatoes, cooked and diced vegetables. Any meat or vegetable will need to be cooked and diced or sliced before being added to the omelette. Depending on your child's age and appetite, a two-egg omelette is usually suitable for one older child or can be shared between two younger children.

## Boiled egg with soldiers

A great favourite of children and adults in the UK. Allow 1 large egg per child. Bring a small pan of water to the boil, with enough water to cover the egg. Add a pinch of salt: this will stop the white of the egg seeping into the water if the shell is cracked. Using a large spoon, gently lower the egg into the boiling water and allow the egg to cook for 3 minutes, so that the yoke is still runny. Remove the egg from the water and place in an egg cup. Cut a slice of buttered toast into strips about 2cm wide. These are known as 'soldiers'. Using a knife or spoon, carefully slice off the top of the egg so that the runny yolk is exposed. Your child then dips the 'soldiers' into the egg and eats the yolk-covered soldiers.

Yummy. The set white of the egg can be eaten using a teaspoon. Tradition says that once the egg is empty the child plays a trick on the parent by turning the eggshell upside down and replacing it in the egg cup so that it looks as if it hasn't been eaten.

## Egg/sausage/tomatoes/baked beans/ cheese/mushrooms on toast

Serve any of these, cooked, on buttered toast for a versatile and wholesome breakfast. Eggs can be fried, scrambled, poached or boiled.

**Fried egg** Melt a knob of butter or butter substitute or a teaspoon of oil in a frying pan. Carefully crack an egg into a small bowl or cup by giving the egg a small sharp tap on the side of the bowl or cup and gently prising apart the two halves of the shell. Slowly turn the egg into the cup or bowl, checking that the egg yolk is whole, and remove any shards of eggshell. Gently pour the egg into the frying pan. Repeat with any additional eggs, keeping the frying eggs separate in the pan. The pan can be covered to accelerate the cooking but check regularly until the desired consistency of the yolk is reached. It takes 3–4 minutes for a medium-set yolk. Serve with the yolk upwards – known as sunny side up – or flip in the pan and cook for another minute for a completely set egg.

**Scrambled egg** Beat together 1 or 2 eggs per person in a bowl with a tablespoon of milk for each egg. Add a pinch of salt and pepper. Beat the mixture for 2 minutes until light and frothy. Melt 1 teaspoon of butter or butter substitute in a frying pan for each egg and tilt the pan so that it melts evenly. Add the beaten eggs and allow them to set slightly. As soon as the eggs start to set, stir gently with a spoon or spatula, gradually lifting and folding the eggs from the sides of the pan so that they don't burn. Repeat until the eggs are softly set and then serve on buttered toast.

**Poached egg**

* If you have a poacher, then lightly grease the cups of the poacher (for however many poached eggs you want – a poacher can usually hold up to 4 eggs) and fill the pan base with water. Replace the lid and bring the water to the boil. Gently crack an egg into a cup or small bowl and check there are no shards of eggshell. Take the lid off the poacher and carefully pour the egg into the greased poacher cup. Replace the lid of the poacher and cook for 3 minutes until the egg white is set. Remove the poacher from the stove. Take off the lid and lift the cup from the poacher. Using a teaspoon, gently ease the poached egg from the cup and serve on a slice of warm buttered toast.

* To poach an egg without an egg poacher, put water in a small saucepan – enough to cover the egg – and bring the water to the boil. Break an egg into a cup or small bowl and check for eggshell. Gently pour the egg into the middle of the boiling water and cook for 3 minutes. Using a large spoon, lift the egg from the water and allow the excess water to drain off. Serve on warm buttered toast.

**Boiled egg** Submerge an egg in a pan of salted boiling water. Cooking time depends on how your child likes the egg. For a medium-size egg allow 3 minutes for a runny yoke, 4 minutes for a firmer yolk (known as a soft-boiled egg) and 6 minutes for a hard-boiled egg, where the yolk and white are set hard. For a large egg, add 1 minute to each of the above cooking times. Once cooked, briefly submerge the egg in cold water so that the eggshell is cool enough to peel and serve on warm buttered toast.

## Eggy bread

Use 1 egg for each slice of bread and break the egg(s) into a bowl. Check there are no fragments of eggshell. Add 1 tablespoon of milk or cream for each slice of bread, and a pinch of salt and pepper to taste. Beat the mixture, using a fork or whisk. Heat a little oil in a frying pan and cut each bread slice in half. Dip the bread into the egg mixture, making sure the bread is covered with the mixture on both sides. Place the eggy bread into the frying pan and cook on both sides until golden brown. Eggy bread is very nice with a splash of brown sauce or tomato sauce, or a teaspoon of relish. For a larger breakfast, serve the eggy bread with one or two of the following: sausage, bacon, baked beans, tomatoes, mushrooms or cold meat.

## Welsh rarebit

A traditional Welsh rarebit recipe includes beer, probably because the dish seems to have originated in eighteenth-century taverns (pubs) in the UK. The beer can be left out when cooking this dish for children. Welsh rarebit provides a healthy and satisfying breakfast, but can also be eaten at any time of the day as a light meal or snack. Here is the child-friendly version, which serves 2:

1 tablespoon oil or a knob of butter

100ml semi-skimmed milk

100g grated cheese

1 teaspoon plain flour

a few drops of Worcestershire sauce

a little mustard (optional)

2 slices of bread, preferably thickly sliced

Put the butter or oil in a saucepan and warm. Add the milk, grated cheese, flour, Worcestershire sauce and mustard. Stir until the mixture is smooth. Remove the pan from the heat.

Toast the bread. Spread the cheese mixture over one side of the toast. Grill until the mixture starts to bubble and turn brown.

Serve on a plate, adding a sliced tomato or salad if desired.

## Toasted sandwiches

These can be eaten as a light meal or snack at any time of the day and they also make a wholesome and satisfying breakfast for children. Cheddar cheese is the most popular filling, but try cheese and chutney, baked beans, cheese and sliced tomatoes, ham, cooked mushrooms, bacon or sausage. If you don't own a sandwich maker, you can lightly toast two slices of bread, add the filling, gently press the two slices of toast together and then warm in a microwave or oven.

## Pancakes

These make a nutritious and satisfying meal to start the day for you and your family when you are enjoying a more leisurely breakfast. Makes 8 pancakes.

100g plain flour
pinch of salt
2 medium eggs
200ml milk
butter, for frying

Sift the flour into a mixing bowl and add the salt. Break the eggs into a cup and check for eggshell. Drop the eggs into the flour and whisk, slowly incorporating the flour. Gradually add the milk and beat the mixture until smooth.

Heat a little butter in a frying pan. Pour about 2–3 tablespoons of the mixture into the pan. Tilt the pan until the mixture covers the base evenly. Cook on a medium heat for approximately 1 minute until the pancake is golden. Flip the pancake and cook the other side.

Repeat with the remainder of the batter.

**Fillings for pancakes** Pancakes are traditionally eaten rolled and with a sprinkling of sugar and lemon juice, but experiment with fillings – savoury or sweet. Try ham and pineapple, spinach and grated cheese, sliced banana, strawberries and honey, blueberries and maple syrup, and for a special treat cream or ice cream (though not necessarily for breakfast).

## Leftovers

Eating up leftovers from the evening meal of the night before, providing they have been stored in a fridge and are thoroughly reheated, can provide a quick, satisfying and nutritious start to a child's day. In my house we are all fans of leftovers and often have to share them. Children usually love leftovers, and one lad I fostered was such a fan that I soon began cooking extra the night before so that he could have the 'leftovers' for breakfast the next morning. Obviously don't store cooked food for more than a day or two in the fridge, but leftovers can be safely frozen, and while you might not appreciate having cottage pie or curry and rice first thing in the morning you may be surprised how many children do.

## School breakfast

Many schools now provide a breakfast for a small charge but what they provide varies, from a bowl of cereal and a drink to a choice of cooked breakfast. Check out what your child's school offers for breakfast and if you don't consider it healthy or worth the money, petition for improvement. It may suit you to use the breakfast club at school sometimes if you have to leave the house early and before your child is ready for breakfast.

## Breakfast for adults

Before we leave the subject of breakfast it is worth remembering that having something to eat and drink first thing in the morning is as important for adults as it is for children. Breakfast kick-starts the body into action by providing energy and fluid to see it through the first part of the day until you have a mid-morning snack or lunch.

# CHAPTER FIVE

# Lunch

Children should eat lunch around midday to ensure they have the fuel and fluid their bodies need to continue functioning efficiently throughout the afternoon. Lunch may be a sandwich lunch or a cooked meal, but it needs to be wholesome and nutritionally well balanced, just as breakfast was and dinner will be. It should not just be a snack of a packet of crisps and a biscuit bar, which will take the edge off a child's appetite but will not give them the essential nutrients and energy they need to sustain them through to teatime or dinnertime.

## School dinner

If your child is at school, he or she will very likely eat a school dinner. In the UK recent legislation means that school menus are now analysed to ensure the food meets minimum guidelines on its nutritional content. A typical day's primary school menu will now offer:

* a minimum of two choices of main course with vegetables or salad, plus potatoes or an alternative carbohydrate such as pasta; in many schools there is a third option of jacket potato with a choice of fillings

* two choices of dessert or fresh fruit
* extra bread
* a vegetarian choice
* a drink, which could be fruit juice, milk or water
* Halal meat certified and approved by the Halal Meat Authority is available in most schools where there is a requirement.

School menus have a cycle of between two to four weeks, and they are changed every term to avoid repetition and to introduce new dishes. Copies of the menu are displayed for parents and children to see, either in the playground or near the school's main entrance.

Secondary schools in the UK usually offer cafeteria-style service, where pupils can choose from individually priced food. As in primary schools, the menus are rotated and the food offered has to meet nutritional guidelines. Vending machines selling fizzy drinks, crisps and chocolate bars – once a feature of many secondary school corridors – have now been removed, and more substantial and healthier snack options are usually available at morning break from the school canteen.

If your child has a school lunch, other than checking that the school is offering an appetizing and healthy menu, and educating your child to choose wisely and therefore eat healthily, there isn't much more you can do to ensure he or she has a good lunch. However, if you send your child to school with a packed lunch, as many parents around the world do, or when your child eats lunch at home at weekends and in school holidays, there is plenty you can do. What your child eats then is solely your responsibility.

# Packed lunch

If children take a packed lunch to school, they usually eat it in the school canteen and lunchtime supervisors are often appalled at what some children arrive with for their midday meal – two packets of crisps and a chocolate bar is not unheard of. While most schools have banned sweets from packed lunch boxes, many snack bars and biscuit bars are just as bad. As well as being low in essential nutrients or having none at all, their high sugar content means they are bad for children's teeth. A packed lunch should be healthy, balanced and nutritious, just like any meal you serve your child, and should contain:

* a drink of water, fruit juice or milk
* a starchy food: for example, bread, rice, potatoes or pasta
* a protein food: for example, meat, fish, eggs or beans
* some dairy produce: for example, cheese, milk or yoghurt
* vegetables, salad and/or fruit

Packed lunches need not be repetitive or boring or limited to sandwiches, but the food you pack will have to be safe to eat when stored outside a fridge. Most packed lunch boxes are not stored in fridges (schools don't have the room); primary schools tend to store them in the canteen or a similar space, while most secondary school children store them in their lockers or carry them in their bags. Insulated lunchboxes are relatively inexpensive and available from most supermarkets; many are designed and attractively decorated for children. In hot weather if you pack a frozen juice box, water bottle or ice pack in the lunch box it will help the food stay cool for longer. It is also a sensible precaution in very hot weather not to pack cold meat or yoghurt. At the end of the day throw away anything that has not been eaten; don't be tempted to put a yoghurt, for example, back in the fridge for tomorrow, as any bacteria will already be breeding.

Here are some suggestions for children's packed lunches.

## Drinks for a packed lunch

It is essential your child has a drink at midday, as otherwise they will start to dehydrate during the afternoon, which will cause them to feel irritable and lethargic, and make concentration difficult. A bottle of water or a packet of milk or fruit juice is fine but fizzy drinks and high-sugar squashes or cordials are not. Explain to your child why it is important to drink during the day, as many children don't take in enough fluid while at school.

## Bread, wraps and rolls

If you regularly make your own bread, fantastic, but if you don't, there is now a huge choice of breads, wraps and rolls available from supermarkets and bakers. Here are some suggestions for you to choose from and alternate between:

**Sliced bread** (for sandwiches) Wholemeal, white, granary, multi-grain, soft or crusty, etc.

**Rolls** Wholemeal, white, granary, seeded, mixed grain, soft or crusty, and in different shapes – round, finger rolls, subway, burger buns, etc.

**Pitta bread** Wholemeal and white, in different shapes and sizes.

**Bagels** Kids love them. Try different flavours and fillings.

**English muffins** Choose from wholemeal, white or cheese.

**Naan** Plain, garlic, kulcha (onion), paneer (cheese), aloo (potato), keema (beef), peshwar (sultanas, coconut and almonds).

**Chapatti, tortilla wrap, fajita** These are flatbreads that make great wraps.

**Croissants** These are soft, easy to eat, and can be slit open and filled like a sandwich, roll or muffin.

## Fillings

Experiment with fillings, but when trying a new one pack a small sandwich or roll with the new filling as well as others you know your child likes. That way they will feel more confident in trying something new. The more variety of foods you give your child, the more likely they will be to try new foods, so ensuring a healthy and appetizing diet. Here are some suggestions for fillings, from the common to the not so common. They are all very simple to prepare and child-friendly.

**Cold meats** Sliced or diced chicken, sliced ham, pork, beef, bacon, salami, sausage, shaved Italian antipasto meats, chorizo and other Spanish cured sausages.

**Cheese** Sliced or grated Cheddar, Edam or any hard cheese; cream or cottage cheese, mozzarella, cheese spreads.

**Fish** Tuna, taramasalata, wafer-thin smoked salmon, prawn cocktail, crab or fish paste.

**Eggs** Hard-boiled and sliced, scrambled, or chopped and mixed with a little salt and pepper, or mayonnaise, chives, dill, onions, tomatoes, cress, chutney, tomato or brown sauce, salad cream or a little curry powder or soy sauce.

**Yeast extract** (Marmite) Children either love it or hate it. Spread very thinly and try it with a slice of cheese or cold meat and salad to reduce the sharpness of the taste.

**Peanut butter** (smooth or crunchy) Again, kids either love it or hate it. Spread thinly and add salad to balance the thickness of the texture. Sometimes schools ask parents not to include nuts or peanut butter in children's packed lunches if a child in the class has a known nut allergy. Respect the request: nut allergies can be very serious. Your child can always have nuts in the evening or at the weekend.

**Hummus** Made from chickpeas, this is traditionally eaten with warm pitta bread, and also makes a tasty and nutritious filling. Spread the hummus liberally inside pitta bread, or use to make a sandwich, wrap or roll.

Add salad to any of the above fillings for extra minerals and vitamins. Choose from and alternate between: sliced or chopped tomato; cucumber; celery; red, green, orange or yellow pepper; lettuce; coleslaw; grated carrot. Add a little chutney, mayonnaise, tomato sauce, brown sauce or mustard if your child likes it. If you mix and match these salads with the above protein-rich fillings and add them to the previously mentioned breads, wraps and rolls, your child will have the calories, starch, protein, vitamins and minerals they need at lunch, for energy and health. Variety is the key to a good packed lunch, and if you rotate different fillings, salads and breads your child could have something different in their sandwiches every day of the year, although they'll have favourites which they'll regularly request.

## Pots

Packed lunches are not only about sandwiches, rolls and wraps, however delicious, nutritious and exciting these might be. They are also about 'pots'. I use the term 'pot' for the little airtight containers that can be filled, and fit into a lunch box and can contain anything from dried fruits to a full meal. They can be used as an addition to a sandwich lunch or instead of one, but don't overload your child with too much food. Pack only what they can reasonably eat at their age, or else your child may feel overwhelmed and eat nothing.

When including a pot that is a meal rather than finger food, remember to pack a spoon or fork for your child to eat with. Check that your child can easily remove the lid of the pot; sometimes when a pot is new the lid fits very tightly. Loosen the lid by snapping it on and off a few times until your child is comfortable doing it. Pots come in different colours and children get very excited about having pots in their lunch boxes. Make the most of

it. Many children who are resistant to eating fruit, salad or vegetables will happily eat it diced and in a colourful pot with their
school friends watching enviously.

## Little extra pots

The food in these pots is in addition to a sandwich lunch or a
main meal pot – see page 62.

**Dried fruit** There is a huge choice of dried fruits now, all of which
are easily available from supermarkets and health food shops.
Dried fruit has a very different taste and texture to fresh fruit
and many children can be persuaded to eat dried fruit in
preference to biscuits. Try: raisins, sultanas, apricots, apple,
cranberries, mango, pineapple, banana, pitted dates and prunes,
mixed dried fruit and yoghurt-coated dried fruit.

**Fresh fruit** Peel and slice or dice 'hard' fruit so that it is ready to
eat straight from the pot. Try: apples, pears, banana, kiwi, orange,
clementine, satsuma, mandarin, grapes, peach, pineapple,
melon. Or try some 'soft' fruit: strawberries, blackberries, blueberries, cranberries, red currants, gooseberries, raspberries or a
combination of any of these. To prevent the fruit from browning
or drying out, sprinkle a little lemon juice and sugar on it.

**Canned and frozen fruit** Most popular fruits can now be found
canned or frozen as well as some lesser-known tropical fruit.
Strain some of the juice from canned fruit before placing a helping of the fruit into the pot. Frozen fruit can be added straight
from the freezer bag, as it will have thawed by lunchtime. Try:

apples, peaches, pineapple, pears, orange or mandarin, grapefruit, lychees, kiwi, grapes, mango, fruit cocktail, prunes, raspberries, strawberries and cherries. Check supermarkets and health food shops for the full range available.

**Nuts** As well as the popular peanuts, cashews and pistachios, try shelled brazil nuts, almonds, hazelnuts, nuts and raisins, or any dried fruit and nuts. All of these can be bought ready shelled in supermarkets and health food shops, but respect any request from the school with regards to nut allergies.

**Salad** Pots can contain one or many different types of salad, chopped and mixed together. Always wash the ingredients first and slice or dice the salad into manageable chunks. The easier a food is to eat, the more likely your child is to eat it at school when time is limited and they would rather be in the playground than eating in the canteen. Try:

* chopped tomato and sweetcorn
* chopped celery and grated cheese
* diced cucumber and tinned kidney beans
* tomato, yellow pepper and pineapple
* cucumber, chives and sweetcorn

Or add a little rice, couscous or pasta to the salad. The possible combinations are endless and the bright colours and variety make for an interesting and attractive salad pot containing the essential vitamins and minerals your child needs. Finish by stirring in a little salad dressing, mayonnaise or any other sauce your child likes.

**Other little pot suggestions** Use what is in your fridge as well as buying specifically for the lunch pots. Try:

* diced cheese and pineapple
* sliced cold cooked sausage and apple
* chopped ham and cucumber
* chopped peppers and feta cheese
* chopped hard-boiled egg and tomato
* grated cheese and coleslaw

And again you can add some pasta, rice or couscous to any of the above, or a little evening meal leftovers, if the meal is nice eaten cold.

## Main meal pots

If the food in the pot is to be the main meal rather than an addition to a sandwich lunch, then pack more food. Use a larger pot if necessary or use two pots.

**Pasta** This is a great favourite with children. It is quick to prepare, easy to eat, and the combinations are endless. Ready-made pasta can be bought from all supermarkets and comes in many shapes and sizes. For pot meals use a relatively small pasta shape: for example, penne (cylinder shaped), fusilli (corkscrew shaped), conchiglie (shell shaped), rotelle (wagonwheel shaped), rotina (spiral shaped), farfalline (bow shaped), or pasta for kids, which includes alphabet- and animal-shaped pasta. Cook according to the instructions on the packet, strain, allow the pasta to cool, and then add any of the following suggestions:

* grated or finely chopped hard cheese
* cream cheese or fromage frais and cooked peas
* chopped cold meat or sausage and cooked sweetcorn
* flaked tinned tuna and very small cooked broccoli florets
* chopped tomatoes or halved cherry tomatoes
* chopped cucumber or celery or grated carrot
* red, green, orange or yellow pepper, chopped
* raisins and chopped nuts
* cooked kidney beans or chickpeas
* chopped hard-boiled egg and tomato
* cooked Quorn pieces and sliced cooked green beans

Add mayonnaise or a salad or vinegar dressing, a pinch of salt and pepper or dried herbs, or any sauce that your child likes, and stir the ingredients together.

**Rice** This is another favourite with children and it is as versatile as pasta. Incredibly there are over 40,000 different types of rice but most of us use no more than half a dozen. For lunch pots use long grain rice (brown or white), which includes the favourite basmati. Boiled rice works better than fried in pots, as fried rice can be dry if not eaten immediately. For each child, put 50ml of rice into a pan with 100ml of water or stock,* and a pinch of salt. Put the lid on the pan, bring to the boil, stir once, cover, turn the heat to the lowest setting and leave to cook – 10 minutes for white rice and 30 minutes for brown. Turn off the heat and leave the rice to cool. You can substitute rice for pasta in any of the above pasta recipes, but don't use mayonnaise or sauce, as it will

---

* As with all references to stock, a stock cube can be used.

make the fluffy rice soggy. Instead, try adding a little curry powder to taste. In addition to the above recipes try:

* rice with diced cooked vegetables and dried herbs
* rice with chopped cooked meat and chives
* sweet and sour rice using small chunks of pineapple and cheese
* rice and curry
* rice with finely chopped nuts and raisins

Experiment: you will find that many of your child's favourite foods can be added to rice to make a delicious rice pot.

**Bulgur wheat** Another alternative to pasta or rice, this is a nutritious wholewheat, and finely ground bulgur wheat is very easy to prepare. It is soaked and not cooked. For each child, put 50ml of finely ground bulgur wheat in a bowl or pan, add 100ml of seasoned boiling water or stock, stir, cover and leave for 10 minutes. Drain off any excess liquid and it is ready to use. Substitute bulgur wheat for pasta in any of the above recipes, and season with fresh or dried herbs or Season-All. Alternatively try bulgur wheat with:

* feta cheese and cherry tomato
* toasted seeds
* dried fruit/beans/chickpeas or cooked vegetables
* diced cold meat and a teaspoon of orange juice mixed in

**Couscous** Made from tiny granules of durum wheat, this is prepared in the same way as bulgur wheat. Couscous can be used instead of pasta, rice or bulgur wheat in the above recipes, or try using it in the following ways:

* added to cooked diced vegetables or cold meat, then seasoned with a little curry powder
* with black beans, kidney beans or tofu – lovely with chopped fresh herbs
* with chopped dates, or any dried or fresh fruit, and a teaspoon of apple juice

Add a slice of wholemeal bread or a roll to any of the above for a lovely combination of taste and texture, rich in essential minerals and roughage.

## Other savouries for a lunch box

As a change from, or in addition to, sandwiches, wraps, rolls or pot meals, try mixing and matching from the following:

* sausage rolls or vegetarian equivalent
* samosa, onion bhaji, pakora
* slice of pizza or quiche
* cheese puff, spring roll or Scotch egg
* breaded chicken or chicken goujons
* mini Cornish pasties or mini pork pies

Crisps and similar snack foods have little nutritional value and should be kept to a once-or-twice-a-week treat rather than included every day.

## Packed lunch desserts

Most children appreciate a dessert in their packed lunch. Try to limit the chocolate biscuits to once or twice a week. Instead, try:

* a yoghurt, jelly or fromage frais
* cold custard, rice pudding or semolina
* a scone, oat cake, hot cross bun or slice of fruit cake
* a piece of fruit, if not included in a small pot

# Lunch at home

Lunch at home allows you greater flexibility in the food you can give your child, with the option of providing a cooked meal. However, there is nothing wrong in giving your child a sandwich lunch at home. If it is nutritionally balanced, as with the suggestions on pages 56–9 for sandwiches, wraps and rolls, it is as good as a cooked meal and better than many fast foods. Also remember that all the pot suggestions on pages 59–65 can be used for lunch at home; simply serve on a plate or in a bowl with a fork or spoon. As most families eat their main meal in the evening, lunch is likely to be a lighter, simpler meal, but eat it at the table as you do your other meals. Even if it is just you and your child, set a good example and eat with him or her at the table and your child will be more inclined to eat healthily. Here are some suggestions for simple cooked lunches that kids love.

## Jacket potatoes

An all-time favourite. Wash and dry 1 large potato per child, prick the skin with a fork, and then rub on a little oil to make it crispy when cooking. Ideally jacket potatoes should be given a long slow cook in the oven, about 1½ hours at 190°C/gas mark 5, but this is uneconomical for one or two potatoes and time consuming. An alternative that works well is to microwave the potato until soft and then pop under the grill for 5 minutes each side to crisp the skin. When ready, split the potato open and fluff it a little with a fork; then add a knob of butter. Here are some filling suggestions:

* baked beans, or baked beans and grated cheese
* bacon or ham and baked beans
* coleslaw, or coleslaw and grated cheese, ham or flaked tinned tuna
* cottage cheese or cream cheese with chopped tomato/chopped apple/cooked sweetcorn/chopped chives
* flaked tinned tuna and cooked sweetcorn with mayonnaise or salad cream
* chopped ham and pineapple with mayonnaise
* leftover bolognese (see page 89), curry (see page 95), chilli con carne or ratatouille
* scrambled eggs with salad cream
* cooked prawns in mayonnaise, salad cream or seafood sauce

Once you have added the filling, serve on a plate with salad.

## Kids' hash

Kids love this variation on corned beef hash. It works well for vegetarians if you replace the corned beef with soy or vegetable protein granules, for example Quorn. This recipe serves 4 and once cooked can be frozen.

1 large potato
1 onion, chopped
oil, for frying
1 x 225g tin of baked beans
100g peas, frozen or tinned
200g corned beef or vegetarian equivalent

Peel the potato and grate it into a bowl. Add the onion and mix together the ingredients.

Fry in a little oil in a pan until soft. Add the baked beans, peas and corned beef. Stir and cook until piping hot.

Serve with bread and butter or a salad.

## Egg in a nest

A simple, fun, appetizing and nutritious lunch.

1 large tomato or pepper (red, green, yellow or orange) for each egg
1 or 2 eggs per child
salt and pepper to taste

Preheat the oven to 200°C/gas mark 6.

Slice the tops off the tomatoes or peppers. Scoop out the inside. Put them into a shallow greased baking dish. Break an egg into the hollow centre of each tomato or pepper.

Cook in the preheated oven until the eggs have set – this should take about 20 minutes.

This is lovely with warm crusty bread and salad. For a different 'egg in a nest', use up leftover mashed potato. Break an egg into the centre of a small bowl of mashed potato, bake as above and serve with baked beans and sliced tomato.

## Stuffed pepper

Many children who don't like raw peppers in a salad enjoy baked stuffed pepper.

1 or 2 peppers per child
salt and pepper or dried herbs to taste

*For the filling, choose from the following:*
boiled rice (pages 63–4) with grated cheese and raisins or
    sultanas
boiled rice, cooked mushrooms and diced ham
breadcrumbs with cream cheese and raisins or sultanas
leftover rice, bolognese (page 89), curry (page 95) or chilli con
    carne
tinned ratatouille or red kidney beans and grated cheese

Preheat the oven to 200°C/gas mark 6.

Slice the top off the peppers and scoop out the seeds inside. Arrange them on a baking tray or deep ovenproof dish. Fill the peppers with your chosen filling and season with salt and pepper or dried herbs to taste.

Bake in the preheated oven for 20 minutes and serve with warm crusty bread.

## Quick cauliflower cheese

If you haven't got the time, ingredients or inclination to make a traditional cauliflower cheese for lunch, try this. Serves 2.

1 medium cauliflower
100g grated Cheddar cheese

Cut the florets from the cauliflower and cook them for 10 minutes in boiling salted water. Drain the florets and arrange them in an ovenproof dish.

Sprinkle over the grated cheese until all the florets are covered.

Place under the grill or in a hot oven preheated to 220°C/gas mark 7 until the cheese starts to bubble.

Serve with a sliced tomato and warm crusty bread or roll.

## Sausage and rice pan casserole

A simple and satisfying winter warmer, loved by children and students. Serves 4. For 2, halve the ingredients or freeze what is left over.

4 sausages (use meatless if you are vegetarian)

oil, for frying

50g long grain rice – basmati works well

1 x 400g tin or carton of tomato soup

Prick the sausages with a fork. Heat a little oil in a frying pan, add the sausages and fry over a medium heat for 10–15 minutes, until cooked on the inside and golden brown on the outside.

While the sausages are frying, cook the rice according to the instructions on the packet.

Drain and slice the sausages.

Remove any excess liquid from the rice and add the tomato soup. Cover the pan with the lid and leave to stand for 10 minutes; the rice will absorb the soup. If after 10 minutes it hasn't, then leave for another 10 minutes.

Add the sliced sausage and stir the ingredients together. Heat thoroughly but do not allow to boil.

Serve by itself or with a salad.

## Soups

A bowl of soup and a roll make a great lunch for kids. Soups are easy to make; you really can't go wrong. There are also many good tinned and packet fresh soups available in supermarkets. Convenience ready-made soups have come a long way in recent years, so don't feel guilty about using them, although some are very expensive compared to soup made at home.

Here are some tried-and-tested recipes for soups that kids love. For a thicker soup, try adding some noodles or dried pasta while the soup is cooking – spaghetti broken into 2cm lengths works well, or any small pasta.

Soup is very versatile and there are no hard and fast rules or ingredients. Mix and match ingredients to suit your child's taste. Add more stock, water or milk if the soup appears too thick, or boil with the pan lid off to reduce the water content.

The following recipes serve 4 and the soup can be frozen.

## Potato and carrot soup

1 tablespoon butter or oil
250g potatoes (1 large or 2 medium), chopped into small
  chunks
2 large carrots, sliced
500ml vegetable stock
300ml milk
fresh or dried mixed herbs to suit your child's taste

Melt the butter or oil in a large pan. Add the potatoes and carrots to the pan and stir so that the ingredients are coated with the butter or oil.

Put the lid on the pan and cook on a low heat until the vegetables start to soften. This will take about 10 minutes.

Add the stock, milk and herbs. Gently cook the soup for another 15 minutes.

Blend, mash or liquidize for a smooth soup or for a chunkier soup leave as it is.

Serve with warm bread or a roll.

**Other potato-based soups** Potatoes make a great basis for any soup because of their starchy texture. Using this recipe, instead of carrots try 2 leeks, or a similar amount of any of the following: courgettes, parsnips, turnip, butternut squash, swede, celery or celeriac, sweet potato, pumpkin. Or combine vegetables using up whatever you have in the fridge. Soups are great for using up odd vegetables.

## Lentil soup

Many children who turn their noses up at the mention of lentils will love lentil soup. As with potatoes, lentils make a great basis for many soups, and lentil soup is especially nice when slightly spiced. Below is a basic recipe, but experiment by replacing the carrots with other vegetables in the same quantity; or try adding some fresh or dried light-coloured fruit, for example apricots or a peeled orange or apple. Don't use dark-coloured fruit, for example prunes, as they will turn the soup an unappetizing colour. Leftover cooked meat – for example, ham, chicken or sausage – can be added, chopped, to the soup for variety.

oil, for frying
1 small onion, chopped
½ teaspoon ground cumin seed or mixed herbs, or a pinch of
    chilli powder (if you want a spicy soup)
2 large carrots, diced
250g split red lentils
750ml vegetable stock or 500ml stock and 200ml milk

Heat a little oil in a large pan and fry the onion, cumin or herbs or chilli powder until the onion is slightly soft.

Add the carrots, lentils and stock or stock and milk. Bring to the boil. Stir and simmer for 15 minutes until the lentils have swollen and softened.

Blend, mash or liquidize for a smooth soup, or for a chunkier soup leave as it is.

Serve with warm naan or a roll.

## Cream of mushroom soup

Children love 'cream of' soups, as they are smooth and comforting to eat, with no strong tastes. This recipe can be used as the basis for any 'cream of' soup by replacing the mushrooms with other vegetables or with cooked meat: for example, cream of chicken soup is a great way to finish up leftovers from a Sunday roast. This recipe serves 4; for 2 halve the ingredients or store the excess in the fridge for a day or two. Not good frozen, as the cream can curdle.

  25g butter
  200g white mushrooms, cleaned, quartered or sliced
  1 onion, finely chopped
  1 teaspoon fresh or dried thyme, or mixed dried herbs
  2 tablespoons plain flour
  400ml vegetable or chicken stock
  100ml double cream

Melt the butter in a large saucepan. Add the mushrooms, onion and herbs and cook for 5 minutes.

Sprinkle the flour over the mushrooms and gradually add the stock, stirring all the time. Bring to the boil and simmer until tender, which will take about 10 minutes.

Remove the pan from the heat and blend, mash or liquidize. Add the cream and heat thoroughly but do not allow to boil.

Lovely served with croutons.

**Cream of tomato soup** Use 750g tomatoes instead of mushrooms and basil instead of thyme.

**Cream of celery soup** Use 8 celery stalks and 1 large potato, all diced. Try adding a little garlic purée or fry a crushed garlic clove with the onions.

**Cream of chicken soup** Use 1 cooked and diced boneless chicken breast or use up leftovers. Add a little garlic and a large diced potato for added taste and texture.

## Pasta lunch

Serve a cold pasta salad using one of the little pot packed lunch suggestions on pages 62–3 or serve a hot pasta dish. Pasta is simple and versatile and can be homemade, or bought fresh or dried from most supermarkets and corner shops. Pasta is an excellent source of energy-giving complex carbohydrates, and teamed with a protein and vegetable sauce makes a perfectly balanced meal. Even kids who are picky with their food love pasta of one type or another. Here are some light pasta meals suitable for lunch at home. If you make your own pasta, cook it for the amount of time given in the recipe you use.

## Cheesy pasta

This is pasta at its simplest but is very popular with children. Serves 2.

    150g dried pasta – penne, rigatoni or similar
    100g grated Cheddar cheese

Cook the pasta following the directions on the packet. Drain and add the grated cheese. Stir over a low heat just long enough for the cheese to melt and coat the pasta.

Serve with salad and garlic bread or a warm crusty roll.

## Macaroni cheese

Slightly more sophisticated than the basic cheesy pasta above but still very simple to make and loved by kids. Serves 2.

    150g dried macaroni pasta (or any similar pasta shape)

    *For the cheese sauce:*
    20g butter
    20g plain flour or cornflour
    300ml milk
    salt and pepper to taste
    100g grated Cheddar cheese

Cook the pasta following the directions on the packet and drain.

To make the cheese sauce, in another pan melt the butter. Add the flour and stir it into the butter to form a roux. Cook for a couple of minutes. The roux should look like a doughy ball. Stir in the milk a little at a time and bring to the boil so that the sauce becomes thick and smooth. Add salt and pepper to taste. Remove the pan from the hob and stir in about 80g of the grated cheese until it has combined with the sauce.

Add the macaroni to the sauce and mix well. Turn the mixture into a deep, suitably sized ovenproof dish and top with the rest of the grated cheese. Place the dish under a hot grill until the cheese is browned and bubbling.

This is lovely served with fresh or tinned tomatoes.

## Tomato pasta

Tomatoes are a very popular base for many pasta sauces but they can also make a pasta meal on their own. Serves 2.

150g dried penne or similar pasta
50g grated Cheddar cheese or a good sprinkle – about 5g – of grated Parmesan
salt and pepper to taste

*For the tomato sauce:*
1 tablespoon olive oil
1 medium onion, peeled and chopped
1 garlic clove, crushed, or ½ teaspoon garlic purée
400g finely chopped tomatoes or a 400g tin of chopped tomatoes

Cook the pasta following the directions on the packet and drain.

To make the tomato sauce, heat the oil in a medium pan and fry the onion for 5 minutes until softened and lightly golden. Stir in the garlic and cook for 1 minute. Mix in the tomatoes. If using fresh tomatoes, cook until soft; if using canned tomatoes, bring to the boil.

Add the pasta and stir well until all the pasta is coated with the tomato mixture. Add salt and pepper to taste.

Turn the mixture into a deep, suitably sized ovenproof dish and top with the grated Cheddar cheese (but not the Parmesan, if you are using it).

Place the dish under a hot grill until the cheese is browned and bubbling.

Remove from the oven and if using Parmesan sprinkle it on now.

Lovely with salad and garlic bread.

**Variation** Try using ratatouille (homemade or tinned) instead of tomatoes.

## Pasta bake

This is a very simple and versatile dish that is another great favourite with kids. A wealth of different foods, to suit your child's taste, can go into a pasta bake. Serves 2.

  1 quantity of tomato pasta (made by following the recipe
    above until the pasta is coated with tomato mixture)
  50g grated Cheddar cheese or a good sprinkle – about 5g – of
    grated Parmesan

*One or two of the following:*

200g cooked sweetcorn

200g cooked peas

200g cooked and chopped green beans

10 cooked and halved button mushrooms

2 cooked sausages, sliced (meatless if your child is
 vegetarian)

4 rashers of bacon, cooked and sliced

200g chopped cooked chicken, ham or other meat

3 hard-boiled eggs, lightly chopped or sliced

200g tinned and drained tuna or salmon

200g cooked prawns

200g cooked fresh fish – for example, cod, haddock, salmon,
 tuna, seabass, halibut, Dover sole or turbot

a similar quantity of any other protein or vegetable your
 child likes

Preheat the oven to 200°C/gas mark 6.

Add the chosen ingredients to the tomato pasta and stir
everything together. Turn the mixture into a deep, suitably sized
ovenproof dish. Top with the grated cheese. Bake in the preheated
oven for 20 minutes.

All pasta bakes are delicious served with garlic bread and a
salad.

## Spaghetti

I have included a recipe for spaghetti bolognese for dinner in the
next chapter (page 89), but your child might like a simpler
version for lunch. Serves 2.

100g spaghetti (approximately)

1 tablespoon olive oil

1 quantity of cheese sauce (pages 76–7) or tomato sauce (pages 77–8)

1 or 2 of the ingredients given in the pasta bake recipe on page 79

a sprinkling of Parmesan cheese (optional)

Cook the spaghetti according to the instructions on the packet. Remove from the heat and drain. Add the olive oil to the spaghetti in the pan and stir through.

Add the cheese or tomato sauce. Return the pan to a low heat and stir until the spaghetti is fully coated with the sauce.

Add the chosen ingredients, stir and heat thoroughly. Top with grated Parmesan cheese, if your child likes it.

Serve with garlic bread or crusty warm bread.

## Tagliatelle

Children love tagliatelle and this very simple version makes a great lunch. Serves 2.

100g tagliatelle

1 tablespoon olive oil

100g grated Cheddar cheese

1 or 2 of the ingredients given in the pasta bake recipe on page 79

salt and pepper to taste

1 tablespoon single cream (optional)

a sprinkling of Parmesan cheese (optional)

Cook the tagliatelle according to the instructions on the packet. Remove from the heat and drain. Add the olive oil and grated cheese to the pasta in the pan. Add the chosen ingredients, stir and heat thoroughly. Season with salt and pepper to taste.

Stir in the cream just before serving, if you are using it. Top with grated Parmesan cheese if your child likes it.

Serve with garlic bread or crusty warm bread.

**Variation** Alternatively instead of the cheese sauce you can use one of the pesto sauces available from most supermarkets. They are tasty if used generously.

## 'Toast lunch'

Eating lunch at home gives you the option of providing a 'toast meal' for your child – that is, cooked food served on toast. A 'toast meal' can be as satisfying and as energy-giving and nutritious as a full meal. Don't limit the toast to just toasted bread: you can also use toasted crumpets, English muffins, halved rolls or bagels. A savoury or potato waffle also makes a great base for a toast lunch. Whatever you use, toast it and then choose a topping from the following (or mix and match):

* scrambled, poached, fried or peeled hard-boiled eggs
* scrambled egg with spaghetti hoops
* poached egg with mayonnaise and chopped ham (a kids' Eggs Benedict)
* baked beans with egg or bacon or sausage

* a stack of sliced cooked sausage, scrambled egg and baked beans
* baked beans with grated cheese on top – pop under the grill until the cheese melts
* cheese on toast or Welsh rarebit (see pages 49–50)

Serve with a side salad or fresh or tinned tomatoes and don't forget the tomato ketchup or brown sauce – essential with a toast lunch.

## Toasted sandwiches

Lunch at home allows you to make the most of the toasted sandwich but don't limit the filling to just cheese. Try:

* cheese and pickle
* cheese and sliced tomatoes
* fried or scrambled egg
* chopped ham or cooked chicken
* sliced cooked mushrooms
* sliced cooked bacon or sausage

Serve with baked beans and a salad for a nutritious and energy-packed lunch.

## Kids' kebabs

It is surprising the foods children will eat (which they wouldn't normally) if there is a novelty factor involved. The kebab is a good example. There is no need to light the barbecue: you can use the grill or oven. Allow at least 2 skewers per child.

> barbecue sauce (bought or homemade), ketchup, brown sauce, soy sauce or seasoned olive oil

*Choose from the following:*
any fresh meat – beef steak, lamb, pork, poultry, kidneys or liver – cubed
Quorn cubes or sliced halloumi
bacon or sausages, sliced
large peeled prawns
potatoes, parboiled for 5 minutes, cooled and cubed
green, orange, yellow or red peppers, sliced
mini corn on the cob (baby corn), cut to the size of the other ingredients
mangetout, cut to the size of the other ingredients
quartered large tomatoes or whole cherry tomatoes
button mushrooms, whole
pineapple chunks, pickled onions or gherkin (if desired)

Thread the chosen food on the skewers. If you have time, marinate the kebabs with one of the sauces for at least two hours before cooking. If you haven't got time, simply coat the kebabs with one of the sauces.

To grill, lay the skewers on the grill rack under a moderately hot grill. Turn so that both sides are cooked, as you would on a barbecue. To cook in the oven, balance the kebabs across a baking tray and cook for 15 minutes in a preheated hot oven (220°C/gas mark 7).

Kebabs can make a meal in themselves, or you can serve them with boiled rice or warm pitta bread. Obviously supervise children with the skewers at all times.

## Bubble and squeak

A quick tasty lunch and a great way to get kids to eat cabbage, Brussels sprouts and many other vegetables, and to use up leftovers. Serves 2.

 25g butter
 1 medium onion, chopped
 1 garlic clove, crushed (optional)
 2 large potatoes, cooked and mashed
 150g (approximately) cooked and finely chopped cabbage, Brussels sprouts, swede, carrots, peas or similar leftover vegetables
 salt and pepper to taste

Heat the butter in a frying pan and fry the onion and garlic until tender. Add the mashed potato and chopped cooked vegetables, season with salt and pepper, and form into patties in the frying pan.

Fry the patties for 5–10 minutes, turning them so that they become golden brown on both sides.

Serve with a fried or poached egg or bacon, sausage, baked beans, mushrooms, tinned or fresh tomatoes. Or top the patties with melted grated cheese or chopped ham.

## All-day breakfast

Don't forget that all the suggestions for cooked breakfast on pages 48–51 also make a great lunch at home for children. Choose from bacon, egg, sausage, tomato, mushrooms, hash browns or fried or eggy bread, or add some salad to a savoury omelette or pancake, for a wholesome and satisfying lunch.

## Lunchtime desserts

Most children will appreciate a dessert at lunchtime, if not straight after their meal then a short while later.

### Fruit

Dessert is a good time to give your child fruit. If he or she is resistant to eating a whole fruit, here are some suggestions:

* Peel and dice fruit and serve it in a small attractive bowl with a tablespoon of cream, yoghurt, ice cream or fromage frais.
* Add some sultanas or raisins to the diced fresh fruit and mix together.
* Serve canned or (thawed) frozen fruit in an attractive bowl with a dollop of cream, yoghurt, ice cream or fromage frais.
* Add diced fresh fruit, canned, (thawed) frozen or dried fruit to a bowl of custard. Ever tried grated apple in custard? It's yummy.

* Fruit in jelly: you will need to make this the night before to allow time for the jelly to set, but if you make several jellies they can be kept in the fridge for a few days.

## Smoothies

Lunch at home means you can give your child a fresh smoothie dessert: for recipe ideas, see pages 42–3. For a lunchtime dessert, you can make the smoothie a bit richer than the breakfast version by adding a tablespoon of cream or ice cream and serve with a spoon.

## Yoghurt

This is another favourite lunchtime dessert with children. However, if you buy pots of yoghurt from a supermarket, as most of us do, rather than making your own, check that it is yoghurt you are buying and not one of the many high-sugar desserts now being marketed in yoghurt-type pots. As mentioned earlier, yoghurt is fermented milk and should contain no more than milk, a bacterial culture (used to allow the fermentation) and a little sugar or fruit, so watch out for large amounts of sugar and any other ingredients unrelated to milk.

## Other lunch dessert ideas

* a mini fruit tart with a spoonful of yoghurt or cream
* a warmed scone or oat cake spread lightly with butter and jam
* toasted tea cake or hot cross bun spread lightly with butter

* a slice of fruit cake
* ice cream, cup cake, chocolate biscuit, chocolate mousse or similar as an occasional treat

## Drinks at home

Provide regular drinks for your child throughout the day. Although you have greater flexibility in what you give your child to drink at home (as opposed to school), the majority of a child's fluid intake should be water, with the occasional squash, juice, milk shake or drinking chocolate, etc. If your child really doesn't like drinking plain water, add a little squash, juice or cordial. With young children who cannot reach to pour themselves a drink of water from the tap, always leave a drink at their place at the table so that they can have a sip whenever they want. It also serves as a reminder for them to drink. Active children can forget to drink and become dehydrated, which can lead to irritability and restlessness.

# Convenience food for lunch

The news is so full of health warnings about processed food that as parents we could easily become paranoid about giving our children convenience or 'fast food'. Nearly all children like a pizza, burger or hot dog, and giving these or similar foods once or twice a week for lunch is not going to do them any harm. It's when every lunch is a processed food (short on nutrients and high in fat) that health problems can result.

# CHAPTER SIX

# Dinner

During the week the evening meal is for many families usually the one meal they are likely to eat together. In addition to being a place for the consumption of food, the meal table provides a social platform on which children and adults can share their news and views. The atmosphere at the table should be light and the interaction as enjoyable as the food served. The evening meal will take into account the adults' tastes as well as appealing to children. Apart from very young children who are being weaned, all members of the family should eat the same food, if necessary with adaptations for children. It is not a good idea to start cooking separate meals for children, for once begun this will be a habit that's difficult to break. Apart from it being a lot of extra work, a child is more likely to eat the food they are given, and thereby eat healthily, if they see their parents enjoying the same food.

As with all other meals, dinner will need to be visually appealing as well as nutritionally well balanced – that is, with protein, carbohydrate, some fat, and essential vitamins and minerals, as described in Chapter Two. After nearly thirty years of cooking dinner for children of all ages, many of whom were fostered and arrived with very poor diets, I'm passing on some suggestions for evening meals that I have found appeal to children of all ages, teenagers and adults. All the recipes in this chapter serve 4.

## Easy and popular main meals

### Spaghetti bolognese

Top of my list must be spag bol. I always cook it when a child first arrives, as I can rely on children and young people liking it. Indeed, I haven't yet met a child (or adult) who didn't like my spaghetti bolognese. For vegetarians, replace the minced beef with soy protein granules.

  2 tablespoons olive oil
  500g lean minced beef
  4 garlic cloves, crushed
  1 large onion, finely chopped
  1 carrot, finely chopped
  2 sticks of celery, finely chopped
  oregano or basil, fresh or dried, to taste
  400g chopped tomatoes, fresh or tinned
  450g tomato purée
  400g spaghetti
  grated Parmesan cheese, to serve

Heat the oil in a large pan and add the minced beef. Stir-fry for about 3 minutes until browned. Add the garlic, onion, carrot, celery and herbs. Cook for another 2 minutes.

Add the chopped tomatoes and tomato purée. Simmer for 15 minutes, stirring occasionally.

When the sauce is nearly done, cook the spaghetti according to the instructions on the packet. Drain it and tip into a warmed serving bowl.

Pour the bolognese sauce over the spaghetti and toss gently or serve on individual plates. Top with grated Parmesan if desired.

## Cottage pie

Coming a close second in my favourites list is cottage pie. This is sometimes also known as shepherd's pie, although cottage pie traditionally uses beef, and shepherd's pie uses mutton or lamb. For vegetarians use soy protein granules.

    2 tablespoons olive oil
    500g lean minced beef
    1 medium onion, finely chopped
    250g sweetcorn, tinned or frozen, or 1 large carrot, grated,
        and 1 stick of celery, finely chopped
    400g chopped tomatoes, fresh or tinned
    2 tablespoons tomato purée
    1 teaspoon dried mixed herbs
    1 tablespoon brown or Worcestershire sauce
    salt and pepper to taste
    800g–1kg mashed potato

Preheat the oven to 220°C/gas mark 7.

Heat the oil in a pan and stir-fry the mince in it for 5 minutes.

Add the onion, and the carrot and celery, if using. Cook for another 5 minutes.

Add the tomatoes, tomato purée, herbs, and sweetcorn if using frozen. Simmer for 15 minutes and then add the sweetcorn if using tinned.

Turn the mince into a large ovenproof dish. Add the seasoning and brown or Worcestershire sauce. Stir through.

Top with the mashed potatoes and place in the preheated oven for about 30 minutes until the top is golden brown.

Serve piping hot with additional vegetables and gravy if desired.

## Lasagne

Another dish that can be relied upon to be enjoyed by children and adults alike. As with all pasta dishes, you have the choice of making your own pasta and sauce or using shop bought. If your family is vegetarian, use soy protein granules instead of minced beef.

25g butter
450g minced beef
1 medium onion, chopped
2 crushed garlic cloves
400g tin of chopped tomatoes
100g washed and sliced mushrooms
½ teaspoon mixed dried herbs (sage, oregano, rosemary, thyme)
400g lasagne sheets

*For the béchamel (white sauce):*
25g butter
25g plain flour
300ml milk
50g grated Cheddar cheese
salt and pepper to taste

Preheat the oven to 200°C/gas mark 6.

Melt the butter in a large pan and fry the minced beef and onion until brown. Add the garlic, tomatoes, mushrooms and herbs. Simmer for about 30 minutes until thoroughly cooked and the sauce is thick. Remove from the heat.

To make the béchamel, melt the butter in a saucepan. Stir in the flour to make a roux (see page 77). Stir in the milk a little at a time and bring to the boil, stirring until the sauce has thickened. Add the grated cheese, salt and pepper.

In a large ovenproof dish layer the ingredients: meat sauce, lasagne sheets, béchamel. Make the last layer béchamel. There is no need to cook the lasagne first, as the pasta will absorb the moisture in the cooking.

Bake in the preheated oven for about 45 minutes.

Serve with a side salad, garlic bread, and a sprinkling of Parmesan cheese if desired.

## Toad in the hole

This was a great favourite of mine as a child. It is cheap and easy to prepare, and always a success with children and adults. Use meatless sausages if your family is vegetarian.

1 tablespoon vegetable oil
8 thick sausages

*For the batter:*
3 eggs
125g plain flour
300ml milk
salt and pepper to taste

Preheat the oven to 200°C/gas mark 6.

Pour the oil into the bottom of a baking dish and arrange the sausages in a single layer. Bake for 10 minutes at the top of the preheated oven.

While the sausages are cooking, make the batter. Whisk together the eggs, flour and half of the milk until smooth. Gradually mix in the rest of the milk until smooth. Season with salt and pepper.

Take the sausages from the oven and pour over the batter, making sure all the sausages are three-quarters covered. Return to the oven and bake for approximately 30 minutes, until the centre is risen and browned.

Serve with baked beans or, if you wish, onion gravy (see page 94).

# Onion gravy

This thick onion gravy goes well with many meat dishes, including toad in the hole and sausage and mash.

2 tablespoons vegetable oil
2 medium onions, chopped
1 teaspoon sugar
1 teaspoon balsamic vinegar
750ml beef or vegetable stock
2 tablespoons plain flour
2 tablespoons milk
salt and pepper to taste

Melt the oil in a large saucepan and gently fry the onions. Cover the pan with a lid and cook slowly until the onions are soft (this will take about 10 minutes).

Add the sugar and vinegar and stir well. Cover and cook for 5 minutes. Add the stock and boil gently, uncovered, for 5 minutes.

In a heatproof jug or bowl mix the flour with the milk until smooth. Pour on a little of the hot gravy and mix thoroughly.

Pour the starch mixture back into the gravy and boil for 10 minutes. This will thicken the gravy. Add salt and pepper to taste.

Serve hot.

## Curry

I have found that even children with quite conservative tastes in food soon enjoy a mild curry with rice and plain naan when they see the rest of the family tucking into it. Curry, rice and naan have a unique appeal in taste and texture; if you fancy a curry nothing else will do. Half a million curries are eaten daily in the UK, so curry is probably now more of a traditional dish than roast beef and Yorkshire pudding. Worldwide there are hundreds of thousands of different curry recipes, although many share the same basic ingredients of coriander, cumin, onion, garlic, ginger, cardamom and turmeric. Below is a basic curry recipe to which you can add cooked meat (500g), vegetables (approximately 500g) or soy protein (300g, cubed) for a delicious and satisfying meal.

3 tablespoons vegetable oil

1 medium onion, chopped

3cm piece of fresh root ginger peeled and grated, or ¼
    teaspoon ground ginger

2–3 garlic cloves, crushed

1 teaspoon ground coriander seed

1 teaspoon turmeric powder

1 teaspoon ground cumin seed

½ teaspoon sugar

½ teaspoon salt

2 tablespoons tomato purée

150ml vegetable stock

Heat the oil in a heavy frying pan. Add the onion and fry for 6–8 minutes, until pale golden. Add the ginger, garlic, spices, sugar and salt, and cook for 1 minute, stirring all the time.

Add the tomato purée and stock and bring to the boil. Simmer for approximately 10 minutes, stirring occasionally, until the curry sauce thickens. Then add the meat, vegetables or soy protein, mix well and cook until heated through. (Remember: if your curry is too spicy, add a tablespoon of plain yoghurt to calm it down.)

Serve your meat, vegetable or soy curry with boiled or fried rice and warm naan. You can use any long grain rice, although basmati is especially good. Allow 60g rice per adult and 50g per child, and follow the instructions on the packet for cooking it.

Ready-made naan can be bought from most supermarkets and is best heated in a medium-hot oven (200°C/gas mark 6) for 10 minutes. Or have a go at making your own. It's not difficult but takes a little time and planning.

## Plain naan

1 teaspoon dried active yeast
1 teaspoon sugar
200g plain flour
¼ teaspoon salt
½ teaspoon baking powder
a pinch of black onion seeds (optional)
1 tablespoon vegetable oil
2 tablespoons plain yoghurt
2 tablespoons milk

Preheat the oven to 200°C/gas mark 6.

Mix the yeast with 1 tablespoon of warm water in a small bowl. Stir in the sugar and leave it to ferment in a warm place for 5 minutes.

While the yeast is fermenting, in another bowl mix together the flour, salt, baking powder and onion seeds, if using. Stir in the oil, yoghurt and milk, and then the yeast mixture, which should be foaming by now. Mix everything together to create a dough.

Knead the dough by making a clenched fist and pressing it repeatedly into the dough. Knead continuously for about 10 minutes until the dough is soft and pliable. Leave the dough in the mixing bowl, cover it with cling film and put it in a warm place to rise for 10–15 minutes.

Divide the dough into four balls and place on a floured surface or board. Roll each one into a long oval shape about 0.5cm thick. Place the dough balls on a greased baking tray in the centre of the preheated oven for 10–15 minutes. They will be ready when they have puffed up a little. Serve hot, straight from the oven.

## Casseroles and hot pots

These are great when you are at home but need to get on with other things. You simply put all the ingredients in a large oven-proof pot and then leave it to cook in the oven. Traditionally a hot pot was topped with sliced potatoes but the distinction between casseroles and hot pots has now blurred. A stew is different in that it is cooked in a saucepan on the hob with the heat beneath, whereas casseroles and hot pots are cooked in the oven and therefore have the heat circulating around them.

# Meat and vegetable casserole

1 tablespoon olive oil

1 medium onion, sliced

2 garlic cloves, crushed

400g cubed meat of your choice (or diced soy protein)

75g mushrooms, washed and sliced

1 large carrot, sliced

1 leek, sliced

2 sticks of celery, sliced

2 tablespoons plain flour

2 sprigs of fresh thyme or ½ teaspoon dried herbs

600ml stock – meat or vegetable

2 tablespoons tomato purée

salt and pepper to taste

Preheat the oven to 200°C/gas mark 6.

Heat the olive oil in a large frying pan. Add the onion, garlic and meat and sauté for 10 minutes, turning so that the meat doesn't burn.

Tip the onion, garlic and meat into a large casserole dish. Add all the other ingredients and stir thoroughly.

Cook in the preheated oven for 1 hour, stirring after 30 minutes.

Serve with potatoes or rice or a large chunk of warm crusty bread.

# Vegetable casserole

400g potatoes, peeled and cut into chunks

2 onions, cut into chunks

3 carrots, thickly sliced

3 sticks of celery, thickly sliced

1 litre vegetable stock

2 garlic cloves, crushed

3 leeks, thickly sliced

150g pearl barley

2 teaspoons dried sage or 1 teaspoon mixed dried herbs

salt and pepper to taste

Preheat the oven to 200°C/gas mark 6.

Put all the ingredients in a large casserole dish and stir thoroughly. Cover with a lid and cook in the preheated oven for 1 hour, stirring after 30 minutes.

Serve with rice or a large chunk of warm crusty bread.

**Variation** Try making this with different vegetables to suit your family's taste: swede, sweet potato, pumpkin, peppers, parsnip, turnip, cauliflower or broccoli florets. For variety try replacing the pearl barley with lentils, rice, beans or dried peas (dried peas and beans need to be soaked first, according to the instructions on the packet). And try replacing the stock with a can of soup for an entirely different casserole but with the same ingredients.

## Hot pot

To create a traditional-style Lancashire hot pot, use the ingredients for the meat and vegetable casserole on page 98. Peel and slice 400g potatoes and arrange them over the top of the dish. Drizzle oil over it and bake in a medium-hot oven (200°C/gas mark 6) for 45 minutes with the lid on and then for 15 minutes with the lid off, until the potato starts to brown and become crisp.

This English hot pot should not be confused with the Chinese hot pot, sometimes also referred to as steamboat, which is more like a fondue.

## Fish and sweetcorn pie

Many children turn their noses up at the prospect of eating fish (other than fish fingers), and I think this is because of the strong smell and taste most fish has. A fish pie is a great way to get kids to eat fish, as the aroma and taste are diluted by the other ingredients. It is very simple to make and appeals to adults and children alike.

400g cod or other white fish
250g cooked sweetcorn, tinned or frozen.
a big squirt of tomato or brown sauce
salt and pepper to taste
1kg mashed potato
50g grated Cheddar cheese

*For the cheese sauce:*
25g butter
25g plain flour
400ml milk
salt and pepper to taste
50g grated Cheddar cheese

Preheat the oven to 200°C/gas mark 6.

Poach the fish by placing it in a pan with enough water or milk to cover the bottom of the pan and simmering for 10 minutes.

While the fish is cooking, make the cheese sauce. Melt the butter in a saucepan. Stir in the flour and cook for 1–2 minutes to form a roux (see page 77). Gradually stir in the milk to form a smooth sauce and then bring to the boil, stirring all the time. Simmer for 5 minutes. Stir in the grated cheese. Season with salt and pepper to taste.

Using a fork, flake the fish, and add it to the cheese sauce. Add the sweetcorn, tomato or brown sauce and mashed potato and season to taste. Stir to combine the ingredients. Turn into a large ovenproof dish and top with the grated cheese.

Bake in the preheated oven for 20 minutes until the cheese is bubbling. Serve with warm crusty bread or warm bread rolls, and an additional vegetable.

**Fish pie variations** As an alternative, choose different fish – for example, haddock, salmon or hake – and try adding a dozen peeled prawns. Also try replacing the sweetcorn with one or two of the following: baked beans, cooked kidney beans, or spinach, sliced leeks, chopped carrots, broccoli or cauliflower florets (all lightly cooked first). And instead of a cheese sauce try using a thick soup; cream of tomato or chicken works very well.

## Stir-fries

I think it is the fun element in this meal that makes it appealing to children: they enjoy the large wok used for cooking and the chopsticks used for eating, although most children will also need a fork to help them eat. Many children who protest at eating vegetables will happily do so when the vegetables are in a stir-fry, especially if they have helped to prepare it by adding the bean shoots etc. to the wok. Stir-fries are nutritionally well balanced; in addition to vegetables they usually contain protein (meat, fish or soya) and carbohydrate – noodles or cooked rice. A word of warning, though: go easy on the soy sauce. Many children don't like it and if you add it generously to the wok you may find a child refuses to eat the stir-fry simply because they don't like the soy sauce. I tend to add a little sauce to the wok to flavour the ingredients and then leave the soy bottle on the table for family members to help themselves. Some children even like tomato sauce on a stir-fry, and what's wrong with that?

Here are some of my favourite stir-fries, which I've found work well with children and adults, starting with the most basic. If you don't have a wok, a large frying pan or saucepan will do the job.

## Simple stir-fry

This very quick stir-fry uses pre-packed bags of vegetables and noodles, which can be bought from all large supermarkets.

2 tablespoons oil
2 garlic cloves, crushed
soy or stir-fry sauce (bought or homemade)
400g chicken, beef or other meat, cut into thin strips, or 200g
    soy protein chunks
600g bag of stir-fry vegetables
600g stir-fry noodles

Heat the oil in a large wok with the garlic and a few drops of soy sauce. Add the meat or soy and cook for 10 minutes, turning the ingredients all the time with the wok spoon.

Add the vegetables and noodles and cook for 5 minutes, turning all the time.

Serve with additional soy sauce as required.

## Simple stir-fry sauce

4 tablespoons lemon juice
60ml vegetable or chicken stock
1 tablespoon soy sauce
2 tablespoons sugar

Combine the ingredients in a jug and stir well. Pour the sauce over the stir-fry at the start of cooking.

**Variations** Try adding a teaspoon of curry powder or dried herbs to the sauce. Experiment with different combinations of spices and herbs to find your family's favourites.

## Beef and baby sweetcorn stir-fry

1 tablespoon oil

2 garlic cloves, crushed

1 medium carrot, cut into thin strips or grated

100g baby sweetcorn, thickly sliced

2 courgettes, thickly sliced

1 yellow pepper, cut into strips

300g beef, cut into very fine strips (for vegetarians use soy
   protein cubes)

1 tablespoon cornflour

150ml beef or vegetable stock

2 tablespoons sugar

2 tablespoons soy sauce

Heat the oil in a wok. Add the garlic, carrot, sweetcorn, courgettes and pepper. Stir-fry for 4 minutes.

Add the beef or soy protein and stir-fry for 5 minutes.

Add the cornflour to a tablespoon of stock to form a paste. Mix
until smooth.

Add the remaining stock, sugar and soy sauce to the wok.
Cook until slightly thickened.

Serve with boiled rice and prawn crackers.


## Honeyed chicken and noodle stir-fry

2 tablespoons oil

2 garlic cloves, crushed

1 onion, thickly chopped

500g chicken, cut into strips (or soy protein substitute)

2 medium carrots, cut into thin strips or grated

1 red pepper, cut into strips

2 tablespoons honey

4 tablespoons soy sauce

500g cooked or straight-to-wok noodles

Heat the oil in the wok. Add the garlic, onion and chicken and stir-fry for 5 minutes.

Add the carrots and pepper and stir-fry for 5 minutes.

In a cup mix the honey with the soy sauce and pour into the wok.

Add the noodles and toss so that all the ingredients are coated. Stir-fry for 5 minutes and serve.

## Other stir-fry ideas

There are thousands of different stir-fry recipes, so don't be afraid to experiment. Try replacing the meat in the recipes above with strips of boneless fish – for example, cod, haddock, tuna or monkfish – or add some peeled prawns. Try adding a handful of nuts to the stir-fry: cashew nuts or water chestnuts work well, but for young children cut the nuts very small or they can be a choking hazard. Mix and match the vegetables; most vegetables work well in a wok if sliced thinly. The ingredients for my stir-fries vary depending on what I have in the fridge. Try:

* sliced mushrooms
* small broccoli and cauliflower florets
* celery
* mangetouts

* different-coloured peppers
* bean shoots, bamboo shoots or shredded cabbage

## Meat and two veg

Many families enjoy a meal of meat and vegetables, arranged in little piles on a dinner plate with lashings of hot gravy.

**Meat** Popular meat for children includes beef, lamb, pork and poultry. Young children in particular often find a large piece of meat on their plate off-putting, as it requires a lot of cutting and chewing. It is therefore advisable to cut meat into manageable-sized pieces, which children can easily fork. The meat can be roasted, braised, stewed, grilled or fried (see the following recipes), but when giving children meat it should be well cooked, a little overdone rather than underdone, to eradicate all bacteria and make it more digestible.

**Vegetables** Many adults like their vegetables very firm, perhaps just blanched, but most children like vegetables to be cooked. However, don't overcook vegetables, as this destroys many of the vitamins and minerals they contain. The best way to cook vegetables such as carrots, peas, broccoli, leeks, mangetout, cauliflower, spinach, etc. is to steam rather than boil them, as this will preserve many of the vitamins and minerals. You can easily steam vegetables without a steamer:

* Boil a little water in a saucepan. The water should be no more than 2cm deep.

* Add the vegetables and replace the lid. Cook for
  5 minutes without removing the lid. The vegetables will
  cook in the circulating steam.
* Remove the pan from the heat, drain and serve.

Choose different-coloured vegetables for variety and to maximize nutritional value – different-coloured vegetables contain different vitamins and minerals.

Here are some child-friendly meat and veg dinner suggestions.


## Roasting meat

Buy the best-quality meat you can afford, as it will be more tender and tasty than a cheaper cut.

Use a large baking tray and place the meat in the centre of a preheated oven. Baste every 30–40 minutes. The cooking times below are approximate and ideally a thermometer should be used to ensure that the meat has been properly cooked.

> *Roasting times (approximate):*
>
> **Roast chicken** 190°C/gas mark 5. Roast for 50 minutes per kg plus 10–20 minutes. Once the chicken is cooked, remove it from the oven, cover with aluminium foil and allow it to rest for 20–30 minutes before serving.

**Roast beef or roast lamb up to 5kg** 220°C/gas mark 7. Roast for 30 minutes at 220°C/gas mark 7. Reduce the oven temperature to 160°C/gas mark 3 and continue to roast for 30 minutes per kg for medium or 40 minutes per kg for well done. Remove the joint from the oven, cover with aluminium foil and allow to rest for 20–30 minutes before carving.

**Roast pork** 220°C/gas mark 7. Roast for 30 minutes at 220°C/gas mark 7. Reduce the oven temperature to 160°C/gas mark 3 and continue to roast for 50 minutes per kg. Remove the joint from the oven and check that the juices run clear, not pink, when you stick a skewer into the meat. Cover with aluminium foil and allow to rest for 20–30 minutes before carving.

**Roast chicken, roast potatoes, peas and gravy** *Tip*: for crispy potatoes and chicken which is not dry, start the potatoes on the second shelf of the oven and the chicken on the top, and then swap them halfway through the cooking time.

**Roast lamb, roast potatoes, baby carrots and sweetcorn** *Tip*: use boneless lamb and then roast with a couple of sprigs of fresh rosemary. Serve with the onion gravy on page 94.

**Roast beef, Yorkshire puddings, roast potatoes, broccoli and sliced carrots** As beef is expensive, this dish is usually reserved for a Sunday treat. *Tip*: although topside is the cut of beef most often used, rib of beef can be more tender. Before roasting rub the joint with olive oil and crushed garlic to draw out the flavour.

**Roast pork with crackling, baby roast potatoes and any root vegetable** – carrots, turnips or parsnips. *Tip*: because pork works well with sweet flavours, root vegetables are ideal, as they become slightly sweet when roasted. Simply peel them, slice lengthways and arrange in the roasting tin around the pork. For crispy crackling, dry out the skin of the pork first by leaving the pork uncovered in the fridge for 30 minutes before cooking and then rub in salt. Score the skin with a sharp knife, which allows the fat to bubble from underneath, making the skin crispy.

## Braising meat

Braise meat in a casserole or hot pot and serve with mashed potatoes: see the recipe on page 98. Because braised meat is cooked for a long time on a low heat, cheaper cuts of red meat can be used: for example, brisket, shoulder (also known as chuck or blade steak), flank, ribs and rump. *Tip*: chicken can also be braised, but use chicken on the bone and leave the skin on for maximum flavour and rich gravy.

## Stewing meat

Stewing meat is another way of providing a meat-and-veg dinner. Ideal stewing beef is usually chuck, leg or brisket. If you are using lamb, choose middle neck or scrag end of neck, and if stewing pork choose belly, shoulder, rib, loin or chump end. Here is a recipe for a simple stew.

2 tablespoons vegetable oil

600g cubed meat

1 medium onion, chopped

1 garlic clove, crushed

500ml meat or vegetable stock

½ teaspoon mixed dried herbs or 2 bay leaves and a sprig of
   thyme

salt and pepper to taste

2 carrots, 2 sticks of celery, 1 large parsnip, 1 medium potato
   (or any other combination of vegetables to suit your
   family's tastes), cubed

Heat the oil in a large pan. Add the meat and brown. Add the onion and garlic and sauté until transparent.

Add the stock, herbs, salt and pepper. Bring to a boil, cover, reduce the heat and simmer for 45 minutes.

Add the vegetables to the pan. Cover and cook for 30 minutes on a medium to low heat, or until the vegetables are tender.

Serve with mashed potatoes, warm crusty bread or boiled rice.

## Grilling meat

Chicken fillet, beef steak or a lamb or pork chop are best for grilling. As with all meat, grilled meat should be cooked right through for children, with no blood juices in the middle. If the adults like their meat rare, then simply remove their portions first and leave the children's meat to grill a little longer. *Tip*: choose thin cuts when grilling meat for children; the adults can have a thicker steak if they wish.

If using a marinade, apply it 30 minutes before cooking; if not, rub a little olive oil and seasoning on to the meat just prior to grilling.

Preheat the grill to the highest setting.

Line a grill pan with aluminium foil for ease of cleaning later. Arrange the meat on the grid of the grill. Place the pan beneath the grill, 5–7.5cm from it.

Turn the meat only once, halfway through the grilling time, to cook the other side.

---

*Grilling times (approximate):*

**Chicken fillet, thighs or legs** 5–6 minutes on each side.

**Beef, sirloin or rump steak** (approximately 2.5cm thick) Allow 1½–2 minutes on each side for rare; 3 minutes on each side for medium; and 4–5 minutes on each side for well done.

**Beef, fillet steak** (4cm thick) Allow 4 minutes on each side for rare; 5 minutes on each side for medium; and 6 minutes on each side for well done.

**Lamb or pork chops** Grill for approximately 10 minutes on each side.

---

## Frying meat

Choose cuts of meat no more than 2.5cm thick for adults and 1.5cm for children. Chops are ideal for frying, as is 'frying steak'. *Tip:* for a tender beef steak, lay it on a chopping board and hit it with a meat mallet or your fist about six times on each side. This breaks down the connective tissue and makes for a more tender steak.

Trim most of the fat off the meat, leaving on a little. If using a marinade, apply 30 minutes before cooking.

If not using a marinade, season with black pepper but leave seasoning with salt until just before serving, as salt can dry out meat in cooking.

Heat a frying pan until hot. Add a teaspoon of oil and heat until hot. Lower the meat into the pan, using a cooking utensil to press down on the meat so that the underside is in full contact with the pan.

Turn the meat once only halfway through to cook the other side.

If the meat has not been marinated, season before serving.

---

*Frying times (approximate):*

**Chicken fillet, thighs or legs** 7–8 minutes on each side.

**Beef, sirloin or rump steak** 1½–2 minutes on each side for rare; 3 minutes on each side for medium; and 4 minutes on each side for well done.

**Beef fillet steak** 4 minutes on each side for rare; 5 minutes for medium; and 6 minutes for well done.

**Lamb or pork chops** Sear first – 2 minutes each side – and then cook for 5 minutes on each side.

---

Remember: whatever the type of meat and the method of cooking, meat for children should be well cooked and cut into manageable chunks. Meat given to very young children should be minced or flaked, and puréed when weaning.

## Puddings

Dinner would not be complete without a pudding, also known as a sweet or dessert. All children love a pudding, and while puddings tend to be high in sugar and fat, as part of a nutritionally well-balanced diet they can be enjoyed, and also provide children with the calories they need for growth and energy. However, as many children have a 'sweet tooth', preferring sweet foods to savoury foods or vegetables and fruit, parents or carers need to serve puddings cautiously and ensure that children don't eat pudding when they have left the main course of the meal. We have a rule in my house that you don't have a pudding until you've eaten most, if not all, of your main course. It's not unkind but it is so important that children get all the nutrients they need, including protein, vitamins and minerals, which are usually present in higher quantities in the savoury part of the dinner than in the pudding.

The pudding you serve will need to appeal to the adults in the family as well as the children. While a 'Yogi Bear' yoghurt might be satisfying for little Emily or Jason, it is unlikely to satisfy the man of the house or older children and teenagers. Here are some of my all-time favourite puddings, which I must have served hundreds of times over the years and which everyone finishes, leaving a clean bowl and requesting second helpings. You could also choose a pudding from the lunch dessert suggestions given on pages 85–7.

# Apple crumble

Top of my list of favourite puddings has to be apple crumble. Delicious, satisfying and wholesome, it is very easy to make. Other fruit apart from apples can also be used: try pears, rhubarb, cherries (stoned), blackberries or gooseberries. Or combine two or three fruits for a seasonal fruit crumble. Fresh fruit is best; canned fruit can also be used but strain off the juices first.

3 medium cooking apples
½ teaspoon ground cinnamon
170g granulated sugar
170g butter or cooking margarine
280g self-raising flour

Preheat the oven to 200°C/gas mark 6.

Peel the apples and cut into quarters. Remove the core from each quarter and slice. Put the apple slices into an ovenproof dish. Sprinkle the cinnamon and 50g of the sugar evenly over the apples.

To make the crumble topping, place the butter or margarine in a mixing bowl. Add the flour and the remaining sugar (120g) and mix, using your hands, a fork or an electric mixer, until the mixture is like breadcrumbs.

Spread the topping evenly over the apples and bake in the middle of the preheated oven for 30–40 minutes, until the top is golden brown.

Serve hot with custard, cream or ice cream. Before eating check that the fruit is not too hot for young children.

# Bread and butter pudding

Another classic British recipe that is a great favourite with children of all ages, and adults of all ages too. Day-old white bread is best but you can use brown bread if you prefer.

8 thin slices of bread
25g butter, plus a little extra (or margarine) for greasing
50g sultanas
1 teaspoon ground cinnamon
350ml whole milk
50ml double cream (optional)
2 medium eggs
25g granulated sugar

Preheat the oven to 200°C/gas mark 6.

Spread each slice of bread with butter on one side and cut into triangles. Grease a 1-litre pie dish with a little butter or margarine. Arrange a layer of bread, buttered side up, in the bottom of the dish. Add a layer of sultanas and sprinkle with a little cinnamon.

Repeat the layers of bread and sultanas, sprinkling with cinnamon, until you have used up all the bread. Finish with a layer of bread.

Heat the milk (and cream, if using) in a pan but do not allow to boil. Beat the eggs with 20g of the sugar until the mixture is pale. Slowly pour the warm milk over the eggs, stirring all the time.

Pour the mixture evenly over the bread. Sprinkle the remaining sugar on top. If possible, leave to stand for 30 minutes.

Bake in the centre of the preheated oven for 40–45 minutes, until the surface is golden brown and the pudding has risen.

Serve on its own or with custard, cream or ice cream.

## Fruit pie

Many people are put off making pies because of the thought of making the pastry. If you make your own pastry, great, but if you don't you can still produce a fantastic 'homemade' fruit pie using ready-made pastry. Pastry – both shortcrust pastry and puff pastry – can be bought from all large supermarkets and comes in ready-to-roll blocks, sheets and cases. I always keep some in the freezer just in case. I'll confess now that the pies mentioned in my fostering stories are usually made from bought pastry, although the ones we enjoy at my mother's are all her own work.

1kg fruit (for suggestions, see apple crumble recipe on page 114)
2 shortcrust pastry sheets, defrosted
100g caster sugar, plus a little extra sugar for the top
1 teaspoon ground cinnamon

Preheat the oven to 200°C/gas mark 6.

Peel, core and slice the fruit as necessary.

Line the base of a pie dish with one of the pastry sheets. Trim off any extra pastry and save it.

Arrange the fruit on top of the pastry. Sprinkle the sugar and cinnamon over it.

Cover with the other pastry sheet, pressing to seal the edge. Trim off any excess pastry and use this, together with the trimmings from the bottom pastry sheet, to decorate the top of the pie with twists of pastry or pastry shapes. Brush the top with a little water and add a sprinkling of sugar.

Bake in the centre of the preheated oven for 20–25 minutes until the pastry is golden brown.

Serve warm with custard, cream or vanilla ice cream.

## Rice pudding

Nothing beats the rich creamy taste of homemade rice pudding. Loved by children and adults, it bears no relation to the lumpy rice pudding many of us remember from school dinners, and little relation to the canned shop-bought variety. Making rice pudding is ridiculously easy but it does need some forward planning, as it requires a long slow cook – 2 hours.

100g pudding rice
25g butter
50g sugar
700ml whole milk
1 teaspoon grated nutmeg

Preheat the oven to 150°C/gas mark 2.

Wash the rice and drain it. Butter an ovenproof baking dish. Place the rice, sugar and milk in the dish and stir thoroughly. Sprinkle on the nutmeg.

Place in the centre of the preheated oven and cook for 2 hours, stirring after 30 minutes and then again after 1 hour.

Serve the rice pudding by itself or with a teaspoon of jam or fruit. Don't forget to scrape off the crispy caramelized skin from around the edge of the dish, which you will need to share out fairly as it is so scrumptious.

Leftover rice pudding can be successfully reheated in the microwave or enjoyed cold.

## Bread pudding

Not to be confused with bread and butter pudding (see pages 115–16), which has a very different texture and taste. This is more of a cake than a pudding, and children love helping to prepare it, as you use your hands and can get very messy.

500g white or wholemeal bread
500g mixed dried fruit
1½ tablespoons mixed spice
600ml milk
2 large eggs
150g sugar, plus a little extra sugar for the top
100g butter, plus some for greasing

Preheat the oven to 180°C/gas mark 4.

Tear up the bread into smallish chunks and place the pieces in a large mixing bowl. Add the dried fruit and spice, and pour in the milk. Using your hands, scrunch up the mixture until all the ingredients are mixed together and form a soggy dough. You can use an electric mixer if you wish.

In a separate bowl whisk the eggs. Add the eggs and sugar to the bread mixture and mix well. Set aside for 15 minutes to soak.

Melt the butter in a saucepan and add to the mixture. Mix well.

Grease a 20cm non-stick square cake tin and add the mixture evenly. Sprinkle the top with a little extra sugar.

Place in the centre of the preheated oven and bake for 1½ hours until firm and golden. Turn out of the tin and cut into squares.

Serve warm as it is, or with a dollop of cream or ice cream.

## Sponge pudding

I guarantee this is the quickest and easiest sponge pudding you will ever make. Loved by adults and children of all ages, it is like a steamed pudding but much lighter.

50g butter
50g caster sugar
1 medium egg
2 tablespoons milk
50g self-raising flour
2 tablespoons of jam, treacle or syrup

Thoroughly cream together the butter and sugar in a mixing bowl. Beat the egg and milk together and gradually add to the butter and sugar. Add the flour and fold in gently.

Put 2 tablespoons of jam, treacle or syrup in the bottom of a microwave bowl. Pour in the batter and cover.

Cook for 3½ minutes on full power, or until the pudding is lightly set.

Serve with custard, cream or ice cream. Children's servings should be allowed to cool slightly so that the jam, treacle or syrup topping doesn't burn them.

## Cake in custard

A naughty but nice pudding which is fine to have occasionally as part of a well-balanced diet. Very quick, very yummy and loved by children and adults alike. Not to be confused with custard cake, which is entirely different. Simply add a couple of slices of plain cake to individual bowls of hot custard and, using a spoon, submerge the cake in the custard. Choose a plain cake; Madeira is ideal or any plain sponge. This recipe is good for using up cake which is a day or so old and perhaps a little dry. Serve as it is or top with a spoonful of cream, ice cream, plain yoghurt or hundreds and thousands.

## Banana and honey whip

Easy to prepare and requires no cooking. Children love to help make this satisfying summer or winter dessert. *Tip*: don't prepare it too long in advance, as the bananas will discolour once peeled.

200ml whipping cream
4 ripe bananas
150ml plain yoghurt
2 tablespoons clear honey
small squirt of lemon juice

Whip the cream in a bowl until light and fluffy. In another bowl slice the bananas and mash well with a fork.

Stir the yoghurt, honey and lemon juice into the mashed banana. Fold this mixture into the whipped cream until blended. Spoon into individual serving dishes.

Serve as it is or top with whatever you fancy – for example, finely chopped nuts, dried or fresh fruit, flaked chocolate, hundreds and thousands, mini marshmallows or ice-cream sauce.

## Cheesecake

Another nice but naughty dessert. This recipe is the simplest cheesecake recipe you'll ever find, but it needs to be prepared 2 hours in advance to allow time for it to set.

200g digestive biscuits
100g butter
600g cream cheese
100g icing sugar
4 drops of vanilla essence
200ml double cream

Crush the biscuits in a mixing bowl. Melt the butter in a saucepan and add to the biscuits. Mix well. Spoon the biscuit mixture into a 20cm loose-bottomed baking tin. Press the mixture down firmly, using a metal spoon. Chill in the refrigerator until set – this will take about 1 hour.

Mix together the cream cheese, icing sugar and vanilla essence in a large mixing bowl. Fold in the cream and mix well.

Spoon the cream mixture evenly over the chilled biscuit base. Return the cheesecake to the refrigerator for another 1 hour until set.

Remove the cake from the tin, cut into slices and serve.

## Trifle

This classic trifle recipe (with juice instead of sherry) is usually reserved for a Sunday treat. There are many variations on this all-time favourite. Try using different fruits, tinned and fresh: for example, raspberries, blackberries, blueberries, pineapple chunks, sliced bananas or kiwi. Try using blancmange or jelly instead of custard, and different decorative toppings, for example chopped toasted nuts, flaked chocolate, fruit segments or hundreds and thousands.

   4–6 trifle sponges or plain sponge cake
   4 tablespoons fruit juice
   250g strawberries, tinned or fresh
   500ml thick custard, shop bought or homemade and cooled
   100ml whipped cream
   3–4 tablespoons blanched flaked almonds, for topping

Arrange the sponges evenly across the bottom of a large glass serving dish. Pour the fruit juice evenly over the sponge. Arrange the fruit over the moist sponge. Pour on the custard and leave in the fridge to set – for about 1 hour.

Once the custard has set, spread the whipped cream over the custard. Top with the almonds or another decorative topping of your choice. Keep in the fridge until just before serving.

# Convenience food for dinner

This could be anything from a complete ready meal to a packet of dried seasoned couscous or a fast-food takeaway. Compared with fresh food, convenience food is high in calories, fats, sugar and salt and is often low in essential vitamins and minerals. But if used occasionally (no more than once or twice a week) and as part of an otherwise nutritionally well-balanced diet, convenience food can save a busy parent time, as well as providing a dish that you might not have made, for example moussaka or samosas. I usually keep a couple of ready meals in the freezer for emergencies. For meals that appeal to children, check out the chiller counter for:

* chicken, beef, Quorn or vegetable curry and pilau rice
* chicken korma or chicken tikka masala
* chilli con carne
* stew and dumplings
* meat or vegetable casseroles
* sweet and sour chicken and egg-fried rice
* cauliflower cheese or swede and carrot mash
* meat or vegetable lasagne
* fisherman's pie
* spinach and ricotta cannelloni
* risotto
* cheese and broccoli bake
* bean and butternut squash crumble

Serve with fresh vegetables or a salad for added nutritional value.

# CHAPTER SEVEN

# Happy snacks

The word 'snack' often conjures up images of chocolate biscuits, sugary snack bars, sweets and crisps, all of which should be eaten sparingly. Many children enjoy a snack between meals and indeed most schools now provide a mid-morning snack to boost children's energy levels (and therefore help concentration) until lunchtime. Snacks need not be sugar heavy and can be just as nutritious as a meal. Here are some suggestions for healthy snacks suitable for home or school:

* a small savoury or fruit pot (for suggestions, see pages 60–62)
* a slice of ham or cheese between crackers
* a small savoury sandwich, wrap or roll
* cream cheese or peanut butter in celery sticks
* a slice of pizza or quiche
* samosa, onion bhaji or pakora
* a sausage or soy-sausage roll
* a slice of fruit loaf, a fruit bun or a scone

And don't forget the drink. Whenever a child has a snack they should also have a drink of water. It is as important to keep the body hydrated as it is to provide it with energy from food.

# Conclusion

In this book I hope I have shown that providing children with appetizing and nutritionally well-balanced meals need not be time consuming or difficult. Variety, moderation and balance are probably the key words for giving children what they need to eat. If your child eats regularly from a wide variety of different wholesome foods, and limits foods that are high in sugar, fat and salt, such as cakes and biscuits, he or she will receive a well-balanced diet containing the essential protein, carbohydrates, fibre, fat, vitamins and minerals necessary for growth and healthy development. Children should be encouraged to eat healthily right from weaning and meals should be eaten at the dining table. Research has shown that if healthy eating habits are established early on children are far more likely to eat healthily as adults, thereby avoiding the many diseases associated with a diet high in sugar, fat and salt, such as diabetes and heart disease. I firmly believe that as parents we are responsible for making sure our children eat healthily. To that end I hope you have found this book useful.

# Acknowledgements

A big thank-you to Anne, my editor; to Andrew, my literary agent; and to Carole, Vicky, Laura and all the team at HarperCollins.

# Cathy Glass

———

**One** remarkable woman, more
than **100** foster children cared for.

Learn more about the many
lives Cathy has touched.

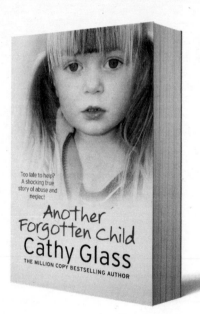

# Another Forgotten Child

**Eight-year-old Aimee was on the child protection register at birth**

Cathy is determined to give her the happy home she deserves.

# A Baby's Cry

**A newborn, only hours old, taken into care**

Cathy protects tiny Harrison from the potentially fatal secrets that surround his existence.

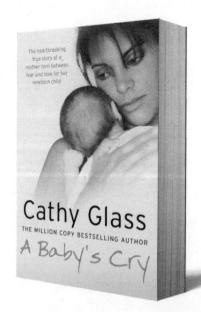

## The Night the Angels Came

**A little boy on the brink of bereavement**

Cathy and her family make sure Michael is never alone.

## Mummy Told Me Not to Tell

**A troubled boy sworn to secrecy**

After his dark past has been revealed, Cathy helps Reece to rebuild his life.

# I Miss Mummy

**Four-year-old Alice doesn't understand why she's in care**

Cathy fights for her to have the happy home she deserves.

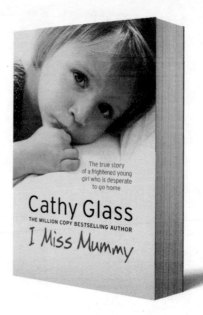

The true story of a frightened young girl who is desperate to go home

## Cathy Glass
THE MILLION COPY BESTSELLING AUTHOR
I Miss Mummy

Cathy Glass
THE MILLION COPY BESTSELLING AUTHOR
The Saddest Girl in the World

The true story of a neglected and isolated little girl who just wanted to be loved

# The Saddest Girl in the World

**A haunted child who refuses to speak**

Do Donna's scars run too deep for Cathy to help?

## Cut

**Dawn is desperate
to be loved**

Abused and abandoned,
this vulnerable child pushes
Cathy and her family to
their limits.

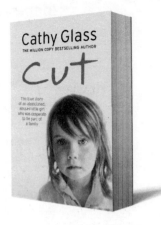

## Hidden

**The boy with no past**

Can Cathy help Tayo to
feel like he belongs again?

## Damaged

**A forgotten child**

Cathy is Jodie's last hope.
For the first time, this abused
young girl has found someone
she can trust.

**Inspired by true stories...**

## Run, Mummy, Run

---

The gripping story of a
woman caught in a horrific
cycle of abuse, and the
desperate measures she
must take to escape.

Cathy Glass
THE MILLION COPY BESTSELLING AUTHOR
*Run, Mummy, Run*
A novel inspired by a true story

## My Dad's a Policeman

The dramatic short story about a young boy's desperate bid to keep his family together.

## The Girl in the Mirror

Trying to piece together her past, Mandy uncovers a dreadful family secret that has been blanked from her memory for years.

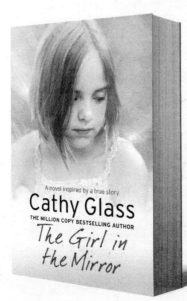

# Sharing her expertise...

## Happy Kids

A clear and concise guide to raising confident, well-behaved and happy children.

## Happy Adults

A practical guide to achieving lasting happiness, contentment and success. The essential manual for getting the best out of life.

## Happy Mealtimes for Kids

A guide to healthy eating with simple recipes that children love.

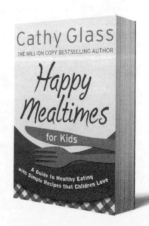

# Be amazed
# Be moved
# Be inspired

---